The Kashfence Philosophy

(Discovering through Rational and Scientific Analysis)

The Kashfence Philosophy

(Discovering through Rational and Scientific Analysis)

Shahin Soltanian

Kashfence Trust Publications

This edition first published in 2020

ISBN 978-0-473-50926-2

A catalogue record for this book is available from the National Library of New Zealand.

Published by Kashfence Trust Publications, Auckland

Contents

Preface

When I was five years old I had a debate with an atheist family member of mine about the existence of God. She was not very good at arguing for atheism and I presented an argument for the existence of God to her which I developed later into what you will read in one of the chapters of this book. Even today I still believe that the argument I presented provides a rational proof for the existence of God. However, at that age, after believing in God I assumed based on what is popular in almost all societies today that the next natural progression was to adopt a religion for myself.

At the time I was living in Iran although I was born in New York, USA. The majority of people living in Iran at the time were Shia Muslims. Although I didn't come from a religious family (but some were religious in my family) the surroundings certainly helped me to accept the Shia version of Islam as my religious belief. Shia version of Islam put special emphasis on using rational reasoning for one's belief and since I would always accept something if I believed it was based on proof and evidence my conviction regarding Shia Islam became stronger. I believed it could successfully show the weakness of other religions while warding off criticism from them.

What never occurred to me until about thirty five years later was that just because one religion is superior in its reasoning ability against other religions, which I believed Shia Islam to be at the time, it is no reason to accept it or any other religion as having a divine origin. I never fathomed the idea of believing in God without religion. To me it seemed belief in God and religion went hand in hand. That belief was a mistake ingrained in me through the cultural practices among almost all societies of our time.

Like proof for the existence of God, belief in a doctrine that claims to be from God also requires rational evidence. To prove something is the word or commandment of God it is not enough that it is superior to other claimants vying for the same title. A religion needs to provide rational and scientific evidence for why a person should dedicate their belief and entire life to living by, propagating and defending its principles and practices. In the absence of such evidence even if one has a rational reason to believe in God there is no reason to follow a specific religion.

The conclusion which I came to through my many years of studying philosophy and the theologies of different religions is that all religions, cults and spiritual leaders who assert to have brought the revealed word of God cannot provide rational and scientific proof for their claim. Furthermore, with proper rational and scientific analysis and the assistance of history one can demonstrate how none can be from God. I have presented my findings in this regards in this book.

In the same way that believing in the existence of God does not necessitate belief in a religion, not having a religion does not necessitate not believing in the existence of God. One does not have to both believe in God and believe in a religion or not have a religion and be an atheist. There is also the option of believing in the existence of a God who caused the existence of everything but has not revealed commandments and guidance in the way the different religions claim. Rather God has placed the intellectual capability in us to discover realities through rational and scientific reasoning. In the same way, the existence of God should only be discovered through rational and if possible scientific reasoning. I am not claiming there are no good arguments for why there is no God (though I present an argument for the existence of God in this work), rather that belief in God does not necessitate having a specific religion or at least one of those religions that have traditionally come down to us throughout history.

Among the reasons why religions have survived through so many years is the structure it gives to the lives of people. Religions usually are comprised of a set of tenets of faith, followed by moral principles to live one's life by and finally by ritual practices for variety of different activities such as marriage and burial practices that is part of what every person does throughout their lifetime. For this reason I did not want to limit the content of this book to just a philosophical position regarding religious belief. I present in this book the Kashfence philosophical guide to living one's life. In this book I have presented a set of principles for belief and practice based not on revelation but on rational and scientific evidence. Furthermore, I have presented a kind of moral guide. This moral guide is through a promise given by a person (let us call them a Kashfenci) to shape one's actions based on justice and what is good with what is just and good being subject to rational and scientific reasoning. In this way I hope to have fulfilled the need for structure in one's life without the need for religion.

I have purposefully not included any kind of ritual practices or definitive instructions of what constitutes justice and what is good so to leave it open to be developed as it has been until now through rational and scientific reasoning as well as deliberation between people. In reality, I am not in a position to instruct people about what is 'good' since what is preferable by one person might not be to the taste of another. There are certain universal principles such as, but not limited to, equality, freedom and the right to not be harmed that everyone would agree or should agree is good and in accordance with justice. But there are preferences to do with sexuality, relationships, nutrition, entertainment and so on that individuals should not be imposing their views on others. If false claims of commandments and word of God does not impose restrictions on what people can eat then the only reason why someone might not eat something could be the scientific findings that prove it to be harmful for their health. Similarly, without religious claims of piety and going against how God intended it to be, consenting adults cannot be restricted from acting according to their sexual preferences.

The Kashfenci philosophy is especially useful for those who believe in a God or creator of the universe but see the problems with claims, practices and instructions of the different religions in existence today. It could also be used by those who don't believe in the concept of God found in many traditional religious teachings.[1]

---

[1] Arguably I have given the same argument for the existence of God as a necessary being which I myself had wrote on previous occasions to have been the same concept argued for by a number of 'Muslim' philosophers. However, the argument for a *necessary being* which is the existential cause of everything given by some Muslim philosophers is not by itself the concept of God argued for in Islam or other religions. The God of Judaism, Islam and Christianity also have certain attributes and either directly or through revelation communicates his commandments and 'guidance' only to certain individuals. The God of the aforementioned Abrahamic religions also has retribution waiting for non-believers. The concept of a *necessary being* however does not have to do any of the things claimed for it by these religions.

Introduction

An important characteristic attributed to the lives of religious figures like Muhammad, Jesus and Moses is the reforms they were said to implement in their respective societies. These individuals seem to have been disturbed by the ills in their society's beliefs and practices and wanted to change it for the better. One could argue that they were at least to a certain extent successful in their goals. Muhammad, for example, was hurt and angry to see the fathers of some of the tribes burying their daughters alive solely because they were girls. Instead of ignoring it, like many others during his time tended to do, he decided to do something about it. It was difficult to convince those for who such practices had become tradition to change their behaviour. So it seems Muhammad thought the best way to achieve such a change was to bring them a commandment from God himself. [2] Jesus is said to have been angry at how a place of worship was being used by merchants and money changers to control and cheat the poor out of their money. He, therefore, started driving the merchants and money changers out. He

---

[2] For Muhammad's concern about live burial of female children and subsequent commandment to stop it see: Quran 81:8-9; 16:58-59.

went on to preach in defence of the poor. [3] Moses is said to have desired to free his people from slavery. This pattern continues with many other religious personalities.

Despite the successes of the personalities mentioned above, it would be unreasonable to attribute divinity to them or their words and even more irrational to require absolute obedience on the basis of those words. I believe that Muhammad, Jesus, Moses and many other religious personalities managed to end or reform some social problems and injustices at least for their own society if not for all humanity. But ending social problems and injustices and contributing to humanity's evolution in thinking and human rights is not the monopoly of religious figures. This is indicated by the fact that the majority of adherents and theologians of Abrahamic religions do not regard other non-Abrahamic religious figures as being prophets of God or having received any divine revelation. Similarly, non-Abrahamic religions are just as dogmatic regarding those who do not follow their system of beliefs and practices. This is despite the fact that the teachings of some of those non-Abrahamic religious figures or non-religious personalities in general can be accepted as being morally valuable and even at times claimed by the very religion that rejects the personalities.

I would even argue that there is a strong possibility that Moses, some Jewish prophets and Muhammad might not have necessarily believed themselves that they were receiving any kind of divine revelation

---

[3] For Jesus driving the merchants and money changers out using a whip see: John 2:13–16.

or commandments and that Jesus did not believe himself to be the son of God. This point would certainly not please the theologians of these religions and invite theological arguments to the contrary of my claim. But let us consider a scenario where these individuals were interested in reforming their society. They probably also believed in a creator God. In trying to reform what they considered to be their societies' ills and injustices they faced communities that had not progressed scientifically and had deeply ingrained superstitious beliefs and practices. The only way they knew how to make any changes in the way their society functioned and conducted their life was to make a claim that appealed to the superstitious nature of that society. For example, there are numerous historical accounts of Muslims during the time of Muhammad questioning his advice or commandments. Muhammad's followers would ask whether a particular directive from him is a divinely revealed directive or one that comes from Muhammad himself. If Muhammad answered it was a divine revelation they would follow through with it whereas if he admitted it was his own directive there was outspoken opposition. In such circumstances it was only natural that Muhammad who cared about making what he considered as necessary changes needed in his society to present the most important of his directives as the very words of God.[4]

---

[4] The Islamic theological argument to counter the suggestion that Muhammad himself might have not believed the Quran was the word of God usually gives an account of Muhammad's reputation as being truthful and honest. He was known as Muhammad the '*amīn*' (trustworthy) who was not known to lie. I do not have any reason to doubt his reputation as being an honest man and I am comfortable accepting the Islamic narrative about Muhammad's character. However a person being generally truthful even if against personal gain is not a proof that he would never lie in circumstances which he would see as being for the good of the general public. The Islamic holy book Quran, which I consider to be the words of

The personality of Jesus also faced social issues which in his time and cultural environment could not easily be argued away by him using rational and scientific reasoning. He had to battle not only superstition but also the stigma of being born out of wedlock (at least as is popularly recorded in historical accounts of Jesus's life).[5] Even if he himself did not create the virgin birth scenario those who followed would have had to justify something so scandalous. To justify a birth of a revered figure out of wedlock it only made sense to cultures that were influenced by prior mythology about gods and their children to attach the title of being the Son of God to Jesus.[6] The biblical narrative also indicates Moses's battle with what he believed to be superstitious beliefs, namely the incident of the golden calf, which in Moses' case if true took an unfortunate and unjustifiably violent turn and ended with three thousand people being killed for their worship of the idol.[7]

Muhammad, encourages what is known as 'taqiyyah'. *Taqqiyah* means that in certain circumstances a Muslim can conceal or lie about his faith among other things. There are also many narrations attributed to Muhammad and other holy figures of Islam that encourage *taqqiyah*. I am not criticizing the concept of *taqqiyah* since I believe that in some circumstances-but not the wide variety found in the practices of many Islamic sects-this is a perfectly reasonable strategy. For example, when lives are at stake, it only makes sense to lie in order to ensure the safety of the individuals in danger. Permission for *taqqiyah* points to the fact that Muhammad believed deception in certain circumstances was justifiable for a greater good. For the permission given to Muslims to conceal their faith in the Quran see: Quran 16:106.

[5]Out of wedlock means Mary gave birth to Jesus without being married. I do not accept the belief in virgin birth but whether a person believes in the virgin birth or not Jesus's conception and subsequent birth was out of wedlock.

[6]Namely, influence from Egyptian, Roman and Greek mythologies.

[7]Exodus 32: 1-29. It should be noted that Moses proceeded to order the mass murder of three thousand people after calming down and advising God not to kill them.

Interestingly, despite the fact that many religions came about through criticism of and a desire to reform the belief systems that came before them their followers feel insulted and some desire to chastise those who criticise their own religion.

Another point raised by those who propagate for revealed religions is that it is because of religion that humanity has its moral codes of conduct. They argue that even if those who do not believe in a religion have moral values they were ultimately brought about by religion and divine commandments. They further reason that without the fear of retribution and promise of reward by God, usually in the afterlife, people would not be inclined to do what is morally good.

The idea that people would only live a morally good life out of fear of retribution or anticipation of reward in the afterlife at most means that a belief in a God that rewards the good and punishes the bad is required not faith in a particular religion or revelation. I will argue that people using their own ability to reason based on rational and scientific proof is a better option for guidance from God than revelation. Furthermore, it is a very weak foundation for living a moral life if one's only reason was to escape punishment and expect reward in the afterlife. It would be much better to encourage people starting with children to live a morally good life because of the reward they will get and the misfortunes they will avoid in this lifetime. Arguing for the intrinsic moral value of certain actions not because someone claims they have heard it from God but because it makes sense seems to be a better way of persuading people to be good. The argument that people will abandon doing what is good without faith in some sort of afterlife assumes good deeds and moral acts are of no use in this life. Otherwise if there are reasons to live a morally upstanding life for this life then there is no need for the threat of what might come in the hereafter. I am not arguing against an afterlife since I have no evidence either way. Rather appealing to the idea of afterlife as a reason for being a good person is in my opinion a weaker point of view than the two views of being good for this life and that moral values are intrinsically good.

The point about religion being the root of moral conduct is baseless. World religions do not have a monopoly on what is morally good. Although there are many laws and codes of conduct in religions that can be argued to be morally good it does not mean that they were first introduced by them. At the very least the followers of a specific religion, who usually reject the teachings of other religions, must admit that their religion did not invent every moral conduct. The idea of not taking innocent lives is something that all human beings of different beliefs and faiths can agree on. Hence, it is not unique to a specific religion. In fact, and I will be giving examples in the future chapters, religious teachings might justify the killing of innocents (as an example, among many others, the story of Moses and the golden calf mentioned above) that otherwise would not be accepted by a rational minded person. Another point to consider is that there are many religions that are not based on any kind of revelation in the Abrahamic sense but which contain some codes of conduct which many can agree to be morally good. Clearly, such codes were the results of the efforts of the thinkers of their respective traditions rather than the words of God.

Finally, whether or not the text and commandment of a religious text contains morally good teachings is not in itself proof that it is revelation from God. Like other sciences that have been accumulated over the centuries with the contribution of different people and cultures, moral conduct too is the accumulation of humanity's endeavour and search to find out what is the best way to live with each other or be good to each other. Humanity's combined efforts and reasoning as well as introspection has led people to accept certain moral principles as being universal. Just as a scientific idea influences societies other than the one it was originally discovered in, ideas about morality also spreads and is adopted among people other than those who originally discovered it.

It is vital to critically analyse the views of different religions because human progress in almost every field relies on personal beliefs regarding the world, humanity's role and position in that world and how a person should interact with the world and other creatures that she shares it with. If a person believes that a rule or a law is from an omniscient God they are less likely to question it and more likely to attempt to move society to comply. Furthermore, he would resist any change in a society that goes against it. But if that belief is baseless then her efforts are not only detrimental to society at large but also to herself and her immediate family and social circles. Belief based on superstition, I argue, is one of the most harmful ways of approaching any issue.[8]

---

[8] I would define superstition as any belief about something external to the mind which is accepted without verification with the exception of rational principles and principles of logic (such as the law of noncontradiction) which will be discussed in the next chapter.

What has been said until now is not limited to Abrahamic religions. Non-Abrahamic religions such as Hinduism and Buddhism also contain superstitious beliefs. In fact, there are many forms of superstitious beliefs that are common in form and substance between Abrahamic and non-Abrahamic religions. In the mid-1990s the Hindu community was gripped by the so called miracle of Ganesh, a deity in the Hindu pantheon. Statues of Ganesh were said to be miraculously drinking milk from the spoon.[9] At the time, the phenomenon caused by the scientifically explicable capillary action, was regarded by many of those who revered Ganesh as a deity, as proof of his divinity. There did not seem to be any interest on behalf of the devout adherents to ask for a scientific explanation or even question the idea why a deity needed to prove his divinity by having his physical representations drink milk. A further question should have probably been asked as to why such a phenomenon would prove the divinity of anything. Similar superstitions can be found in Abrahamic traditions, such as names of Allah in natural structures for Muslims, the bleeding of trees during Ashura for the Shia Muslims and Jesus and Mary's faces and names on toasts and other objects.[10]

Sometimes such superstitions could be mostly harmless with the exception of engraining false ideas in the mind of the believers (which arguably could later lead to harm). However, there are many beliefs and

---

[9]Tim MacGirk, "Hindu world divided by a 24-hour wonder," *Independent*, September 23, 1995, https://www.independent.co.uk/news/uk/hindu-world-divided-by-a-24-hour-wonder-1602382.html.

[10]The phenomenon of the bleeding tree can be explained either by the red colour of some tree saps or watering a tree with coloured water beforehand.

practices that are harmful to people and society. The caste system practiced dogmatically among many adherents of the Hindu pantheon is an example of a belief that is blatant abuse of human rights. Similarly, views of many religions regarding sexuality and sexual orientation, place of women in society and even bodily function related to women (such as their periods) are examples of superstitious beliefs that do cause harm to individuals and society.

Hence, in this work I have also dedicated a chapter to Hinduism and critically analysed some of the beliefs and practices associated with the Hindu pantheon.

1   Rational and Scientific Reasoning

Any kind of reasoning is based on the belief that there are things which exist other than what is in one's own mind. Hence, one needs to verify whether a statement is true about something external to one's own mind by seeing if it corresponds with what is in reality. In other words, it must be the case that outside of one's own mind the belief is actually the case and is not subject to or dependent on what is in the mind. Verification of a belief regarding an external reality (i.e., it is the case independent of one's mind) can only be achieved through evidence. Evidence shows us whether a statement is subjective and only in a person's mind or objective and therefore true regardless of what is in a person's mind. This evidence can take the form of sense perception or other rational and scientific proofs and analysis.

There are some exceptions to the general rule of verifying through evidence what is outside of one's mind through the methods of sense perception, rational and scientific analysis. There are some beliefs that are true without verification and which all other verifications and evidence is based on but are rational nevertheless. An example of a belief which is true without verification is the belief in the truth of the Law of noncontradiction. To be more specific such principles as the principle of contradiction that states that conjunction of contradictories is impossible does not need and cannot be verified. The truth of such principles or belief in the truth of such beliefs is innate within each individual and maybe even animals on a rudimentary level. Animals go back to where they left a hunt expecting it to still be there not both be and not be there at the same time. [11] I would suggest that there is no need to verify such principles as the principle of contradiction due to the fact that its objective verification is included within one's self and mind. The verification is the mere existence of our self and mental existence. Our existence and our consciousness while we exist and the fact that we are not non-existent demonstrates innately to us without having a need for proof that the principle of contradiction is true since we cannot both exist and not exist at the same time. Although this evidence is our very own mind it is nevertheless objective and rational.

Not everyone agrees with the idea that knowledge of certain principles such as the principle of noncontradiction is innate. In some epistemological writings, it has been asserted that the principle of contradiction can be acquired empirically. Albert Casullo, for example, states that the knowledge of principle of contradiction can be acquired through experience. He asks us to imagine a person who sees five fingers at one time and does not see those same five fingers at another time (say, he sees four fingers). Casullo concludes that from such an observation one can know that some statement is not both true and false. Hence, in this way, the principle of contradiction is acquired through sensory observation. Casullo states:

---

[11]I am not saying animals understand the principle of noncontradiction as a logical principle. Rather, animals innately and consciously expect the world to behave in a way that we would regard as following the principle of noncontradiction.

Suppose, for example, that Hilary believes on the basis of looking at his hand that the statement "My hand has five fingers" is true but, when he looks again, he discovers that his hand has only four fingers. The subsequent observation that his hand has only four fingers justifies him in believing that the statement "My hand has five fingers" is false and that the statement is not true. Hence, his faith in the belief that the original observation report is not both true and false should remain unshaken since the subsequent observation also justifies that belief.[12]

Casullo is incorrect. All that the observation of five fingers at a particular time confirms is the existence of the five fingers at that particular time. Similarly, all that not seeing five fingers (i.e., seeing only four fingers) at a particular time confirms is the non-existence of those five fingers at that particular time. How one could come up with the principle of contradiction from these two observations is not demonstrated by Casullo. There is nothing in these observations alone that suggest that in a totally different situation one cannot observe the five fingers as both existing and not existing (i.e., as both being five and four) at the same time. Moreover, if one is going to rely on observation alone, one cannot even rule out the possibility that in the situation described by Casullo it is the case that there are and there are not five fingers at the same time. There is nothing in the observation alone that can justify the claim that it is not the inability to comprehend that things can both exist and not exist that gives one the impression that things have

---

[12]Albert Casullo, "A Priori Knowledge," in *The Oxford Handbook of Epistemology*, ed. Paul K. Moser, New York: Oxford University Press, 2002, 110-111.

to either exist or not exist. After all, if one is going to rely on observation alone, then seeing five fingers on one's hand and then four fingers on the same hand should be a good reason for the possibility that there are and there are not five fingers on the same hand. Hence, Casullo's example fails to show that the knowledge of the principle of contradiction can be inferred by the observation of things existing and not existing at the same time.

In fact, the truth of the two observations cannot be confirmed without accepting the truth of the principle of contradiction. If it was the case that things could both exist and not exist at the same time, then there is nothing ruling out the possibility of the five fingers not existing when they are seen as existing and the five fingers existing when they are not seen. For this reason, not only there is no indication that the two observations produce knowledge of the principle of contradiction, but their status as knowledge would not be justified without knowledge of such a principle being true.

This latter point signifies the importance of the principle of contradiction in regards to any knowledge that one might have. It also indicates that any argument (whether a priori or empirical) put forward to justify or negate this principle would assume the truth of this principle.[13] An argument always has premises and a conclusion. If the premise/s is both true and false at the same time, then the conclusion will also be true and false at the same time. Hence, the premise/s has to be either true or

---

[13]A priori knowledge is based on theoretical deduction rather than empirical observation. However, I have expanded the meaning of a priori to mean any knowledge that does not need empirical observation including axiomatic truths.

false. The principle of contradiction is used when it is assumed that the premise/s cannot be both true and false at the same time. Consequently, it is not only the case that the principle of contradiction is a priori but also that it is necessary, it cannot be revised (whether based on empirical justification or through a priori reasoning) and its scope of application is universal.

The scope of application of the principle of contradiction is another reason why this principle is not empirical. This is mainly because as noted before, empirical findings are particular and can only make judgments in regards to what has been observed. General propositions inferred from empirical findings can only apply to those things observed and whether or not they apply to other than those findings is a mere guess. For this reason, general propositions that are inferred from empirical findings, even though are assumed to apply to other than the observed facts, can be proven wrong if a particular case can be found which can escape its application. It is for this reason that general propositions discovered empirically are said to be revisable. Is it, however, reasonable to think that such a case can be found in regards to the principle of contradiction? Casullo seems to think so. He states:

> How can we rule out the possibility that some future physical theory, perhaps one that we cannot now conceive, might imply the denial of MPC *(minimal principle of contradiction)* but nevertheless be accepted because it explains a diverse range of phenomena,

yields surprising predictions that are subsequently verified, and enhances our understanding of the world?[14]

It has to be asked, however, how it is that at one time the principle of contradiction will be proven to be false if the truth of the conclusion of the physical theory depends on the acceptance of the principle of contradiction. Take, as an example, W.V.O Quine's criterion for an empirical process to be justificatory. According to Quine, a process is justificatory if it satisfies a system of beliefs such as simplicity, familiarity of principle, scope, fecundity and testability of experimental results. Quine states:

> The benefits thus credited to the molecular doctrine may be divided into five. One is simplicity: empirical laws concerning seemingly dissimilar phenomena are integrated into a compact and unitary theory. Another is familiarity of principle: the already familiar laws of motion are made to serve where independent laws would otherwise have been needed. A third is scope: the resulting unitary theory implies a wider array of testable consequences than any likely accumulation of separate laws would have implied. A fourth is fecundity: successful further extensions of theory are expedited. The fifth goes without saying: such testable consequences of the theory as have been tested have turned out well, aside from such sparse exceptions as may in good conscience be chalked up to unexplained interferences.[15]

---

[14]Casullo, "A Priori Knowledge," 110. Italics mine.
[15]W.V.O Quine, "Posits and Reality," in *Ways of Paradox and Other Essays*, Kingsport: Random House, 1966, 234.

Let us call Quine's criterion, φ. For there to be any purpose for φ it has to be accepted that it can justify beliefs. If it is both the case and not the case that φ can justify a particular belief, then φ is no different to any other absurd criteria, especially since it would also be the case that those absurd criteria can both justify and not justify a particular belief as well. Hence, the principle of contradiction is assumed in proposing φ as criteria for justification. Note that, as was stated above, the principle of contradiction is not only significant in regards to the justification of beliefs but also in regards to justification of beliefs regarding sensory information.

If the principle of contradiction is denied, then there is no basis for denying that the so called finding from physics is both true and false. Since the principle of contradiction is considered false, then the finding is both true and false (since it does not have to be the case that it is on either side of the contradiction). Hence, it is both true and false that the principle of contradiction is false.

In some philosophical writings attempts have been made to avoid the aforementioned conclusion by suggesting that it is the case that the principle of contradiction is both true and false. It is true in regards to some things and false in regards to others.

Such an assertion, however, is flawed. For example, consider the following:

(2)	The principle of contradiction does not apply in context A.

Now, either it is the case that the principle of contradiction does not apply in context A or it is not the case (even someone asserting (2) will usually agree that it cannot be both). If it is the case that the principle of contradiction does not apply in context A, then it cannot be the case that the principle of contradiction does apply in context A. However, the principle of contradiction is applied to context A when it is stated that either it is or it is not the case that the principle of contradiction does not apply to context A. Hence, by stating that the principle of contradiction does not apply to context A, it is assuming that the principle of contradiction does apply to context A. This argument shows that there cannot be any situation or case where the principle of contradiction is false or does not apply.

Now suppose, as some dialetheists have done, that the principle of contradiction can both apply and not apply to some context A, contrary to what was assumed above.[16] This assertion, however, also implicitly assumes that the principle of contradiction 'does' apply, and that it is not the case that it both applies and does not apply. The reason for this is that either it is the case that the principle of contradiction both applies and does not apply or its contradiction is true (i.e., it is not the case that the principle of contradiction both applies and does not apply), thereby assuming the truth of the principle of contradiction. Hence, the assertion that the principle of contradiction both applies and does not apply to context A is really an assertion that the principle of contradiction does apply to context A and it is not the case that the principle of contradiction

---

[16]Dialetheism is the belief that there can be a true statement whose negation is also true.

does not apply to context A. Consequently, the original motivation that the principle of contradiction both applies and does not apply to context A is undermined by the mere assertion that the principle of contradiction both applies and does not apply to context A.

One has to keep in mind that even if the aforementioned conclusion does not follow (which is difficult to see how), then the dialetheists still need to show why it is the case that the principle of contradiction applies in one context but not another. In reality, rejections of the principle of contradiction rely on there being more than two truth values. For example, a proposition can not only be true or false but also true and false or neither true nor false. However, even such an assertion would assume the principle of contradiction and as a result show the implausibility of its claim. Assume that there is a third truth-value true&false other than the truth values of true and false. In a given case, something either has the truth-value true&false or not and it is not the case that it both has and has not the truth value true&false. This 'either has or not but not both' disjunction points out that the truth of the principle of contradiction is assumed.

It might be objected that since any argument for the principle of contradiction assumes the principle of contradiction, then there is no way to justify the truth of the principle of contradiction. Any attempt to do so would be circular.

Certainly, it is true that arguments presented for the principle of contradiction assume the principle and consider contradictions to be false. On the other hand, it is not true that the arguments are being given as a 'reason' for the falsity of contradictions or that it is being used as an argument for the truth of the principle of contradiction. The purpose of such arguments is only to bring to attention that all contradictions are false, not to provide a reason for such a proposition. This is because, as it was mentioned above, any argument given for or against the principle of contradiction must assume the principle of contradiction. Hence, no argument can be presented to prove the principle of contradiction.[17]

Casullo proposes another interesting empirical method for acquiring knowledge of the truth of the principle of contradiction. He states:

> For example, a student may believe that MPC is rationally unrevisable solely on the testimony of a philosophy instructor. But, if the student's justification for believing that MPC is true is based on the justified belief that MPC is rationally unrevisable then, if the latter belief is justified a posteriori, the former is also justified a posteriori.[18]

The issue that Casullo seems to have overlooked is whether it is possible for the student not to have knowledge of the truth of the principle of contradiction so that she acquires that knowledge through the

---

[17]Note that even the objection that arguments for the principle of contradiction are circular assumes the principle of contradiction. For if one is to argue against any argument by calling it circular, one has to be committed to the principle of contradiction. If one is going to reject circularity as plausible (which I too reject it with them), then they will have to assume the principle of contradiction as being true. Circularity is either plausible or not in any given case. If it is both plausible and not plausible in a given case, then the given case would be both plausible and not plausible. Hence, it is assumed that circularity is not both plausible and not-plausible.

[18]Casullo, "A Priori Knowledge," 111.

testimony of the teacher. Furthermore, if the student does not have knowledge of this principle then, on what basis can she accept the testimony of the teacher? In reality, the student needs to have knowledge of this before she accepts the testimony of the teacher about its unrevisability (since, the truth of the testimony depends on this principle), even if it is implicit and not known in the form of a logical proposition. This is because, as it was stated previously, anyone who believes in the truth of any proposition assumes the truth of the principle of contradiction. Hence, the student already has knowledge of the principle of contradiction and all that the testimony of a teacher could do is draw the attention of the student to what she already knew. If it was the case that the student did not have knowledge about the principle of contradiction, the teacher's testimony cannot be a justification for her to believe it.

It is important to point out that some dialetheists have attempted to present arguments for the negation of the principle of non-contradiction in regards to at least some cases.[19] Their arguments focus on such paradoxes as the Liar Paradox. The liar paradox can be presented in the following way:

(*): (*) is not true

Sentence (*) is problematic because if one claims that it is true then it would also be the case that it is false. On the other hand, if one claims

---

[19]Graham Priest, J.C. Beall, and Bradley Armour-Garb, ed., *The Law of Non-Contradiction: New Philosophical Essays*, New York: Oxford University Press, 2004.

that it is false then it is the case that it is true. Hence, dialetheists conclude that there are cases where something is both true and false where the principle of contradiction does not apply. Responses to such paradoxes as the Liar Paradox vary in their presentation but seem to be similar in their ultimate aim that propositions that are inherently contradictory refer to nothing. However, before noting the responses, it has to be said that the Liar Paradox is not a criticism against the main point that has been emphasized in this chapter, namely, that the principle of contradiction is known without empirical observations. It was already mentioned that even claims that there are cases where the principle of contradiction does not apply would have to assume the truth of the principle of contradiction on a local level. If the dialetheist assumes the principle mostly applies (for example, in all places except those 'at the limit of thought'), then the arguments presented for why it cannot be the case that one empirically acquires knowledge of the principle of contradiction still stands.

This is not to say that we should acquiesce in the views of dialetheists. Among the solutions presented that attempt to preserve the principle of contradiction is that cases such as the Liar Paradox cannot be assigned with a truth value. The claim, of course, is not that the Liar Paradox is neither true nor false and therefore both true and false, but that it is a case where because of the inherent contradiction present in them they cannot be assigned a truth value. Such propositions are vacuous. In other words, such sentences as (*) are not statements because they state nothing. In this regard Laurence Goldstein states:

So, initial appearance to the contrary, 'This statement is not true' is not a statement; it states nothing; in particular, it does not state that it is not true. Do not be fooled by the presence of the phrase 'This statement'—the description 'the number that is four less than itself' does not describe a number. Similarly, the token of the sentence 'S is not true' mentioned above does not yield a statement; it has no truth value. It has a character, but no content; it is discontent.[20]

Among other approaches to the Liar and similar paradoxes is the view that such paradoxes at best show that there is a fictional element involved in our use of the predicate 'true'. Frederick Kroon in his paper *Realism and Dialetheism* states that at most such paradoxes can be credited with providing reasons for us not to be a realist about discourse that generates true contradictions.[21] Kroon argues that paradoxes such as the Liar Paradox show that some of our conceptual tools are defective at certain points. Hence, these conceptual tools cannot be used to fully represent the real world. Explained in this way, contradictions that seem to be true do not show that the world is inconsistent but that our conceptual tools are not fully adequate to represent the real world. He states:

> This way of understanding the phenomena of 'true contradictions'
> puts the blame on our conceptual tools; it removes, or at any rate

---

[20]Laurence Goldstein, "The Barber, Russell's Paradox, and More," in *The Law of Non-Contradiction: New Philosophical Essays*, ed. Graham Priest, J.C. Beall, and Bradley Armour-Garb, New York: Oxford University Press, 2004, 303.

[21]Frederick Kroon, "Realism and Dialetheism," in *The Law of Non-Contradiction: New Philosophical Essays*, ed. Graham Priest, J.C. Beall, and Bradley Armour-Garb, New York: Oxford University Press, 2004, 245-263.

mitigates, the tendency to think that the world might itself be inconsistent in some way.[22]

Other than such innate principles that demonstrate the truth of all our beliefs regarding reality anything else needs to be verified. Verification of what is true and what is not outside of the mind needs evidence. Such evidence can take many forms. Sometimes our senses might be sufficient to verify a belief. In such cases our sensual perception is a rational evidence for something being true. However, there are many cases such as hallucinations where the senses are not capable of verifying reality. The intent of this book is not to delve in detail into the epistemological discussions regarding all verification methods of what constitutes knowledge. Such discussions are appropriate for a book on the subject of epistemology. The important point to emphasize is that a belief needs evidence and that evidence must be either through pure rational arguments (which I believe the proof of existence of God falls in this category) or through scientific analysis (which includes within it rational evidence). Outside of these two methods (rational and scientific) belief in something external to the mind is at best a lucky guess and/or superstition.[23]

---

[22]Kroon, "Realism and Dialetheism," 254.

[23]It can be a lucky guess as well as a superstitious belief if the belief happens to be true by chance but the basis for accepting that truth is superstition. For example, take a person who believes that oranges (the fruit) are good for preventing the flu because they are the colour orange and that the colour orange has special powers. Even though oranges might turn out to be good for preventing the flu (the lucky guess) it is because of their for example, vitamin C content, and not special powers of the colour orange (assuming colour orange does not have special powers).

I would use the term 'superstition' for any belief about something external to the mind which is accepted without verification with the exception of rational and logic principles such as the law of noncontradiction mentioned above. One must train one's mind so that not to give into superstitions. There are many psychological reasons why a person might cling to a belief despite not having rational and scientific evidence for it. For example, social pressure and the desire of a person to be liked or favoured by his peers might reinforce and instil superstitious beliefs accepted by the person's peers. The desire to be correct in one's claims, fear of the unknown, vanity and ego are among other reasons that could persuade a person to keep to a superstitious belief. Another reason a person might keep to a belief despite having no evidence for it is the privileges that belief brings with it (such as in cases of racism, sexism, etc).

The idea that one must believe in the truth of a claim based on rational and scientific evidence is opposite to the basis of religions that require belief in their truth based on revelation, word of God (or a spiritual leader having access to the occult) and/or faith. Some religions, such as Islam, claim to have rational evidence for their claim of revelation from God and the truth of that religion. However, as it will be discussed in later chapters, when rationally scrutinised the evidence provided by Islamic theologians of various sects cannot prove the conclusion they wish to achieve.

Other religions, such as Christianity, require their adherents to believe in the truth of their claims based on faith. The problem with believing through 'faith' alone is that it is both circular in trying to prove its claim as well as by definition in contrast to belief by rational evidence. Religions that propagate their ideas through faith alone intend to block the path of rational proof and evidence for proving their claims. Promoters of belief through faith usually approach the issue in two ways. They either assert that God creates the spiritual condition in a person that results in the intended religious belief or they require an absolute trust in God or a spiritual leader to show the person the 'righteous' path. Both these methods of believing require a person to retire, at least for the purpose of believing, their natural tendency to ask why something is the case and closing the doors for rational evidence.

In cases where it is God that creates the spiritual condition for a person to become an adherent of a particular faith then there is no need for rational evidence. It is God that makes someone into a believer. Such a deterministic way of thinking then would require belief in an unjust God that favours some over others. Since many religions also contain ideas of reward and punishment in an afterlife (usually eternal in nature) then the God that does not bestow the favour of belief on some is not a just and good God at all. The same criticism applies if it is argued, as some Islamic theological schools do, that God produces in people the spiritual condition to accept evidence provided for a belief but withholds the same spiritual condition from others. In either case, the freedom to choose based on evidence is kept from the people.[24] There is also the problem of circular reasoning when it comes to belief through faith by the spiritual condition

---

[24]If the claim is that God creates the ability of rational reasoning in individuals to freely accept what is correct then this criticism does not apply. However, there is a difference between having the ability to freely reason and analyse evidence and God having created a spiritual condition to accept evidence.

God creates in a person. If the reason for arguing for a religious belief is that God creates the spiritual condition needed to believe then both the existence of God and the method he will use to guide his followers is assumed.

Another approach is to encourage people to believe by trusting a spiritual leader or a prophet. At times this trust is based on the testimony of the spiritual leader or the prophet. Testimony can be a rational reason for arguing something is the case. Much of world's judicial systems depend on testimony of individuals. However, if testimony was to be accepted as rational evidence for religious claims then the same level of scrutiny (if not more) that one finds in a court of law should be applied to the testimonies of spiritual leaders and prophets. However, most religions and religious figures not only are not subjected to the same level of examination that one finds in a court of law but their doctrines usually forbid it in one form or another.

Furthermore, it is never sufficient to accept the testimony of a person who claims to have contact either with God or the supernatural since what is disputed is the very claim itself. Hence the person making the claim needs to bring independent proof other than his or her testimony for his or her claim.

2   Existence of God

There are different types of causes for something coming into existence and for events which occur. For example, one type of cause is that which gives form and shape to something but the thing itself can continue to exist without the need for the cause that gave it its form and shape. The carpenter is the cause that gave form to the table but the table might continue to exist long after the carpenter's death. However, for the purpose of a rational evidence for the existence of God we need to consider the 'existential cause' of things. The argument for the existence of God needs to see if there is a need for an existential cause for everything other than God itself. Existential cause is what causes something to be (to exist) and continues to sustain the existence of that thing. Take for example, the act of turning a key in a lock. The cause of the existence of the key turning is the hand which continues to give it existence. When the hand ceases to turn the key the existence of the turning of the key stops (the key is no longer turning).

When one contemplates over one's surroundings, then one realizes that although they currently exist it is possible for them not to exist and at some point they may have not existed. Such things or beings will be termed in this writing as contingent beings.[25] If it was not possible for something not to exist (existence was necessary for it) then it would have had to always have existed and would continue existing. Such a being (which I will argue one of which can only exist), I will call for the purposes of this writing a 'necessary being' (a being that exists by necessity). A *necessary being* which has always been existent and has never not existed has no need for a cause to exist as that would require it to have not existed at some point and then brought into existence by a cause.

Since a contingent being can either exist or not exist and therefore existence is not necessary for it, in order for it to exist it would need an existential cause to bring it into existence. A contingent thing cannot be an existential cause for itself since if it already existed then there was no need for it to be brought into existence in the first place. A temporal delay cannot solve the paradox of a contingent being bringing itself into existence because an existential cause needs to continuously sustain the existence of its effect as explained above.[26] The existential cause of a contingent thing can also be contingent and this could go on *ad infinitum*. However, if the existential cause of a contingent thing was also contingent then it too would need an existential cause and so on *ad infinitum*. Given that an existential cause must continue to sustain the existence of its effect there cannot be a temporal delay between the

---

[25] I am not claiming to have invented the term or the definition but want to make it clear how the term will be used here.

[26] By temporal delay I mean the idea that A caused B to exist then went out of existence itself and then B again caused A to exist then went out of existence which again caused B to exist and so on.

existential cause and that which it has brought into existence. The need for contingent beings to have an existential cause that brought them into existence and sustains their existence is not alleviated because such a chain of causes continue to infinity. In fact, the entire infinite chain now needs an existential cause. Take for example, an infinite number of light bulbs wired together so that each one would receive electricity from one before it in order to turn on. The number of light bulbs even if it goes on to form a series of infinite light bulbs does not alleviate their need for electricity to be run through them to turn on. Electricity is something they do not have from themselves. Similarly, a contingent being that does not have existence from itself and needs it from another then if the other is also contingent that need now applies to both contingent beings and so on ad infinitum. The difference between contingent beings and the light bulb analogy is that the light bulb has existence and needs only electricity whereas the contingent being needs an existential cause for everything to do with it existing.

Since contingent beings of themselves cannot exist and need a cause which has brought them into existence and sustains their existence then that existential cause must be a *necessary being* (a being that exists by necessity) and does not have a cause for its existence. This *necessary being* is God.

The next issue to consider is whether there can be more than one *necessary being* and whether it is comprised of or can be divided into parts. Rational analysis indicates to us that it is not possible for the necessary being to be comprised of parts since if it was comprised of parts it would be the parts that have brought it into existence and continue to sustain its existence making it being a *necessary being* redundant and a contradiction (it would be both a necessary being and not a necessary being). To demonstrate the aforementioned points let us consider several possibilities. One possibility is that the *necessary being* is comprised of at least some elements that are contingent. Take EP to be that which is comprised of necessary existence and something else. Take E to represent the necessary existent component of EP and P to represent the something else with contingent existence. E existentially precedes P, as it is the case that P's existence is dependent on E. Hence, E is the true *necessary being* that necessitates and sustains P and every other contingent being. Then, P must be included in the totality of other contingent things and not as part of the *necessary being* that is their cause.

E and P cannot have a separate existence to EP (i.e., the combination) because it was assumed that E and P are both part of an entity known as EP which has necessary existence and is the *necessary being*. The existence of P must then either be necessitated by E or something else. If it is necessitated by something else then EP's existence and therefore E's and P's existence is dependent on something else to necessitate and sustain its existence which is contradictory to the original claim that EP has existence by necessity and is a *necessary being*. EP's existence must therefore be dependent on its parts E and P. For EP to exist, E must necessitate and sustain P. This means that for EP to exist, E must necessitate and sustain EP since EP's existence is dependent on E necessitating and sustaining P. Because it was assumed that E and P exist together as one being and not separately, E's existence is also dependent on EP and therefore dependent on P. Therefore, for E to necessitate P, EP and as a consequence P must first exist. If P already exists then there is no reason for E to necessitate and sustain its existence. In addition, at least E was assumed to have necessity of existence on its own and without the need of anything, including P, to necessitate and sustain its existence.

In other words, for E to necessitate and sustain the existence of P, EP (i.e., the combination) and as a consequence P must exist first in order to cause and sustain the existence of E and P. Similarly, for EP to exist, E must first necessitate and sustain P and as a consequence EP. EP must therefore precede its own existence and necessitate and sustain its own existence. The impossibility of such a proposition is clear by considering both the fact that a thing cannot precede its own existence and that in order for EP to exist it must both precede its own existence and not precede its own existence. The reason that a *necessary being* cannot be comprised of two component parts one of which is necessary in its existence and one of which is contingent is due to the fact that they are contradictory to each other. A being which is comprised of component parts one of which existence is necessary for it and one of which is contingent and needs an existential cause both exists through itself and through another (i.e., another has necessitated and sustained its existence). This, however, is impossible. The above proof indicates that impossibility.

Other possibility that should be considered is that it could be that the *necessary being* is composed of parts that can exist independently of the whole and each other or they can only exist with the whole. If the parts can exist independently of the whole then the existence of the whole is necessitated by its parts in which case the whole does not have existence itself and is not a *necessary being*. It could be argued that the parts can exist independently of the whole then, the whole needs a cause to have necessitated and sustained the joining of the parts. The parts are either contingent in their existence or existence is necessary for them and they are all *necessary beings*. If the parts have contingent existence then, the same argument which was given for why a series of possible beings need a cause outside of itself to necessitate and sustain its existence, can also be given in this case. If, however, the parts are all independently *necessary beings* then the argument is directed to whether or not there can be more than one Necessary Being.

The assumption, however, can be made that the parts cannot exist without the whole and the whole cannot exist without the parts with the whole necessitating the existence of the part and the part necessitating the existence of the whole. Take EQ to represent the whole and E and Q as the parts of that whole. For EQ to exist by necessity (not having a need to exist and never not have existed) its existence must be necessitated and sustained by E and Q, since both E and Q have necessary existence and cannot be the effect of the other. But for E to exist EQ must necessitate and sustain its existence. Similarly for Q to exist EQ must necessitate and sustain its existence. The result is similar to that of EP, in the sense that something must both precede and not precede itself in existence in order to exist and remain in existence. Moreover, E must become the existential and by the definition given above the sustaining cause of the existence of Q and vice versa even though it was assumed that E and Q are *necessary beings*. The *necessary being*, therefore cannot be comprised of parts in any sense.

Rational analysis also concludes that there cannot be more than one *necessary being*. In other words, everything else other than that one *necessary being* has contingent existence. The assumption that there is more than one *necessary being* requires that they have in common with each other the fact that they have necessity of existence. Each one must also have a specific difference that separates it from the other *necessary being* for otherwise without a distinguishing feature there is no basis to say that more than one entity is the extension of the concept of a *necessary being*.[27] The specific difference of each *necessary being* is either that which is a condition (i.e., is a cause) for the necessity of their existence or not. Clearly, it is not a condition for the necessity of their existence for otherwise every *necessary being* is in need of that feature in order to have necessity of existence. If every *necessary being* has that feature then again we arrive at the situation where one being is not distinguished from the other. It must therefore be the case that necessity of existence is an accidental feature of that specific difference. However, the impossibility of the assumption that necessity of existence can be an accidental feature of the *necessary being* has already been shown above. It was shown that if existence is not necessary for something then it is contingent in its existence and in need of a *necessary being*. The only

---

[27]Note that occupying different spaces is not a viable option for distinguishing more than one *necessary being* since space is contingent in its existence. In either case that which comprises of space is composed of parts and therefore not a *necessary being*.

other option is to claim that the necessity of existence is part of the identity of each *necessary being* with the other part being different between each of the necessary beings. Then, the part which is different either has necessity of existence or is contingent in its existence. It was shown that in either case the two cannot be instantiated in reality due to the contradictions that arise from both assumptions. It was also shown that circular causation is impossible and therefore it cannot be the case that the first *necessary being* is the cause of the possible element of the second *necessary being* whereas the second *necessary being* is the cause of the possible element of the first *necessary being*. Therefore, more than one Necessary Being cannot exist.

Another argument can be given for why there cannot be more than one *necessary being*. Let us take X and Y to be two *necessary beings*. X has a certain level of perfection, namely, X-ness, which Y, being completely different to X, does not have. In such a case, X's existence is limited by not having Y-ness and Y's existence will be limited by not having X-ness. Limitation is something added to the existence of the *necessary being* in the sense that what one *necessary being* does not have is what identifies and distinguishes it from the other *necessary being*. This, however, means that the *necessary being*'s existence is dependent on something it does not have since it is that which it does not have which distinguishes it as what it is in itself. In a manner of speaking, it is comprised of two component parts, what it has, namely, X-ness and what it does not have (i.e., Y-ness). That it is a composite and that it is dependent on what it does not have is not only contradictory to having necessity of existence but also makes each one dependent on the other.

X's existence is dependent on the component parts of X-ness and not having Y-ness. Not having Y-ness, however, is dependent on Y. A similar circumstance applies to Y. Hence, the two are dependent on each other. But it has already been shown that circular causation is impossible. It must then be the case that there cannot be more than one Necessary Being.

It might be argued that X is distinguished from Y not by what it does not have but by what it does have, namely X-ness. However, what distinguishes X from Y cannot be just X-ness because it can always be argued that X-ness is Y-ness and therefore there is no difference between the two and they are one and the same thing. Hence, X must be comprised of X-ness and that X-ness is not Y-ness. If it is further argued that one *necessary being* must then also be limited and comprised of parts because it has necessity of existence and not contingency of existence. In response to this, it can be argued that not having contingency of existence is having necessary existence and therefore not a limitation or a composition. It is simply a negation of a limitation. In the case of two *necessary beings*, however, because both have been assumed to have necessity of existence and an attribute not shared by the other, then the negation of what it does not have is necessarily an indication of limitation not a negation of limitation. That is, Y-ness is not a limitation but a kind of perfection and similarly X-ness is not a limitation but a kind of perfection. Therefore, due to the impossibility of circular causation and a *necessary being* having dependence on another, it must be the cause that two necessary beings cannot be instantiated in reality. There is, therefore, only one *necessary being*.

The extension of a single concept can only be a single reality. Anything else that implies multiplicity is something added to that concept. For example, the extension of the concept of 'human being' includes more than one human being only because concepts such as place, time and other such concepts are added to it. The *necessary being* cannot have anything added to its reality for that would imply that its reality and therefore its existence is caused (i.e., necessitated and sustained) by another which is contradictory to being a *necessary being*.

When considering that the *necessary being* is the cause of all contingent beings and all that they have then any kind of ability (or perfection), such as knowledge and consciousness for example, cannot be denied from it. Anything that is the result of need which is the attribute of a contingent being is therefore rationally denied from it. Hence, it can be argued that the *necessary being* is omnipotent and omniscient.

3   Critical Analysis of Revelations and Prophets of God

Many religions claim that God has communicated to people through revelation. Such revelations are usually transmitted through an individual known as a prophet or a messenger. According to some religions, for example Islam and Judaism, revelation can also be transmitted to the chosen prophet or messenger through intermediaries such as angels. Theologians that belong to religions that consider revelations from the divine as an integral part of their doctrine have presented different arguments for the need and existence of such revelations. When examining their arguments several fundamental underlying questions can be identified. These questions need to be answered through rational means before claims regarding the need or existence of revelation from the divine can be confirmed. The following are five such questions:

1) Why is there a need for a revealed word or guidance from God?

2) Why is the word and guidance of God only sent or revealed to a few?

3) What proof or evidence do individuals claiming to have received the word or guidance of God have for their claim?

4) Can those claiming to have received guidance or revelation know for certain that such a revelation is from 'the God' rather than other possibilities?

5) Is there any evidence that can rationally and scientifically demonstrate that the revelations and words of God claimed by a particular religion are in fact not from God?

I will show that religions that claim to have divine revelations fail to give adequate and convincing answers to the above questions if analysed through rational and scientific methods. Furthermore, their reasoning and claims cannot withstand the criticisms that demonstrate the words and revelation that they claim to be from God is not from God.

Probably the best attempt at giving a rational argument (as opposed to appealing to faith or tradition) for why there is a need for revelation and guidance from God is found in the religion of Islam. The argument for such a need is refined further in the Shia sect of Islam.[28] Islamic theologians have argued that God has a purpose for creating something and has not done so in vain. Hence after accepting the existence of God and deducing that he is good and just and wants the best for his creation then there is two options. The first option is that God has created human beings and then left them on their own to figure out what is good on an individual and societal level. Ordinary human beings

---

[28]See: Hasan b. Yusuf b.'Ali Ibnu'l-Mutahhar Al-Hilli, *al-Bābu 'l-Hādī 'Ashar (A Treatise on the Principles of Shi'ite Theology)*, London: The Royal Asiatic Society, 1928, 54-6. For a comprehensive summary of the Shia Islam's theological views see: Wahid Khorasani, *Tozīh al-Masā'el* . Qom: Madrese Bāqer al-'Ulūm, 1381 H.S., 52-6.

however have defective reasoning ability and lack knowledge regarding ethics, morality and what is right and are swayed by their whims and desires. This places human beings at a disadvantage of not being able to figure out the true guidance from God because of having defective reasoning ability and lack of knowledge which is affected by desires. The second option is that God has sent guidance through revelation (*wahy*) to teach human beings and their defective intellect what is good and bad, what is proper and abhorrent and what is just and unjust so that they can achieve the reason for which they were created, that is, to become the best that they can be and enter heaven. It is then argued that the revealed word of God teaches people how to achieve the best way of living both in this world and in the hereafter. It is also free from being defective because it is from God and therefore also not tainted by personal human desires. Shias develop this further by realising that if the messenger of God is himself swayed by desire he will not be able to deliver the message correctly. So the Shias attribute infallibility to their holy figures, Muhammad and his family. The Sunni sect of Islam generally only attributes infallibility to Muhammad in regards to delivering the revelation.[29] Since, God is gracious and wants the best for his creation just as he has given guidance to all of his other creations, for example, by teaching the bee how to make honey, he would out of his grace (*lutf*) do what is best for human beings and reveal guidance for their defective intellect. According to the Islamic theological arguments God would not

---

[29]Though this seems to be not the only view from a traditional perspective since there are narrations attributed to Muhammad that claim the Islamic Satan might have influenced some verses that were revealed to him known as the satanic verses.

withhold guidance through revelation because that would be against God's perfection of doing what is best.

It seems that the abovementioned argument assumes that human beings are less capable and advanced than even the bee. God has supposedly placed guidance within all his creation, for example the bee, without need for an external source. The guidance for the bee is innate. Human beings, on the other hand, need guidance from someone else that also is not deserving of having it himself but rather can only attain it through revelation through an angel.[30] Many Islamic theologians might argue that the kind of revelation the bee receives is not the same as the guidance sent to prophets and messengers. However, this does not resolve the main problem that human beings with more advanced intellectual capability are regarded as unworthy to be guided innately.

In Islamic theology there exists a concept known as *ilham* or a divine inspiration. Inspiration unlike revelation can be received directly by individuals especially if those individuals have earned it through spiritual purification. Revelation on the other hand is physically and mentally too demanding for the mind of simple people who are not chosen by God. Distinctions such as the one between revelation and inspiration seem to

---

[30]Shia Islamic theologians have argued that prophets and Imams are infallible and have an innate ability and knowledge of what is right and wrong some going as far as claiming that they have knowledge of every kind of science regarding the universe and what is contained in it. If that is the case then there is no reason to claim that they need external revelation. They are perfectly capable based on their knowledge of discerning what is right and wrong. The prophets and Imams with such abilities should be able to guide humanity without the need for revelation. Historical evidence and arguments that will follow below, such as ignorance regarding certain scientific and geographical facts, show that in fact they did not have such abilities at all.

be attempts by polemics to defend why revelation is sent to only a few 'chosen' individuals. No other evidence other than the claim of the religion itself, in the above case Islam, can be given for distinctions between for example inspiration and revelation. It seems such distinctions were conveniently created, usually by later theologians and polemics of a religion, to justify the limitation of guidance in the form of revelation to only a few.

Furthermore, the same theologians that lay out what is the best and most gracious way for God to guide human beings put aside the idea of a gracious God when it comes to the problem of evil. In other words, such theologians do not include the idea that God considers all possible actions and only acts in the way best for his creatures when presented with the problem of evil. The problem of evil asks why it is that God does not do what is best for his creation in cases of natural disasters. Some have extended the problem of evil to include actions of tyrants and criminals which God allows to happen rather than preventing it. The argument of evil states: If there is an omnipotent, omniscient and good God then he should prevent all evil. If there is evil in the world then either God is not all good and therefore does not prevent evil, or is not omniscient and does not know how to prevent it or is not omnipotent because he cannot prevent it.

In regards to evil committed by tyrants and criminals the argument is that for freewill to exist then God must allow individuals to be free in their actions including their evil actions. Religions such as Judaism, Christianity and Islam claim the wrongdoers will see retribution and their victims will be compensated in the afterlife through damnation for the former and eternal bliss for the latter. In reply to why it is that God allows or is the cause of natural disasters, some of the very same theologians who argue for why God's grace necessitates revelation reason that ignorance of the true reason for such natural disasters is why we cannot see the final good in them.

It is possible to construct an argument for why there is no need for revelation or chosen people to bring people the word of God through the same reasoning theologians use to justify why God can cause natural disasters but still be omnipotent, omniscient and all good. It can be argued that God has given people an innate ability to figure out through rational and scientific reasoning what is right and wrong. There is no need for any external guidance especially through few chosen individuals. If that innate ability is not perfect it does not mean that it is not the best way God could have guided human beings. Rather, it only means that we are ignorant of the reason for why it is the most gracious way God guides human beings. This argument refutes the idea that there is a need for revelation through Prophets and Messengers using the same argument from ignorance used to justify natural disasters which theologians use to answer the problem of evil.

In reality it seems to be more gracious and a much better way of doing things if God guided people through their own ability to reason rather than an external ambiguous source. The sources of guidance in different religions include holy books, words and actions of certain individuals. These sources need exegesis and explanations through more ambiguous and unreliable sources. For example in Islam, Quran is said to be the direct words of God revealed to Muhammad. Several barriers are placed in front of a Muslim to receive the guidance supposedly contained in the Quran. First, he must know the Arabic language and the historical meanings, metaphors and references that are unique to the language at the time of the revelation of the Quran. Second, Quran on its own without explanation is ambiguous and needs explanation through exegesis that references the actions and words of Muhammad (the *sunnah*) and in case of the Shias the *Ahlul Bayt* (family of Muhammad). To properly interpret the actions and words of Muhammad (and in case of Shias the *Ahlul Bayt*) again a person needs to know the Arabic language, the historical context of a particular action or statement and verify the authenticity of attributing such an action or statement to its source. The effort to acquire the true Islamic guidance from the divine sources has led to the development of various different subjects to properly verify and identify the word of God.[31] Judaism and Christianity also need to verify any claim of revelation or commandments of God if it were to be applied. This process would require some study and interpretation of the original language of the divine text and the historical contexts of its commandments and parables.

Religions that are not faith based and require some level of reasoning to accept its guidance ultimately rely on the ability of an

---

[31]Examples of such subjects: science of narrations/tradition (*Ilm al-hadith*) which studies the transmission of narrations and traditions from a holy figure such as Muhammad or one of the *Ahlul Bayt*; science of biographical studies (*ilm al-rijal*) which investigates those who reported a specific narration or tradition; study of exegesis or interpretation of the Quran (*ilm al-tafsīr*) which investigates the context of a revelation in the Quran.

individual to choose the 'right' path through reasoning. It does not seem to be the best course of action for God to place such barriers for receiving guidance rather than innately guiding every human being. It is such barriers that throughout history conveniently create a class in a society called theologians who make their living through the study of the subjects needed to 'identify' the word of God. A counter argument can be given that even in a secular society there is a need for a group of people to analyse ethics, morals and laws to establish whether they are in accordance with justice and protection of people's rights. However, the difference between the two is that in a secular society individual experts gather to analyse and debate what is good for society through their innate reasoning ability assisted by rational and scientific evidences available to them. The interpreters of God's words, on the other hand, are tasked with deriving their conclusions through ambiguous divine commandments with no basis in rational and scientific findings. Therefore, a moral, ethical and legal conclusion derived from rational and scientific reasoning is much better guidance on how a society should function than a conclusion derived from ambiguous commandments without any solid evidence other than the claim it is divine.

In addition, if defective knowledge and reasoning ability affected by desires is the reason for needing divine guidance then the same argument can be given for identifying and interpreting that guidance. The same defective ability has to be used to identify and interpret what is divine guidance. That raises the possibility that the defective ability is not capable of identifying and interpreting guidance from God or to do so correctly or completely. If the reasoning ability of human beings is sufficient for identifying and interpreting guidance from God then it seems redundant, unnecessary and more burdensome and therefore less gracious to require individuals to identify and interpret through an external source of guidance rather than an inner ability to reason through rational and scientific analysis. If the ability to reason would be tainted by desires if no guidance is sent by God, unless the very same messenger is available to people at all times the same ability would be tainted when identifying and interpreting God's guidance. Arguments could be presented that many theologians are indeed tainted through desires to interpret divine commandments according to what benefits them. The argument given by many Muslim theologians fail to show that there is a need for guidance through revelation and prophets. In fact, a gracious God should do what is best for His creatures and make guidance easier and based on more solid evidence by guiding through people's own innate reasoning ability.

Having a solid rational and scientific basis for moral, ethical and legal decisions becomes even more crucial when considering that the religious opinions have very significant consequences when it comes to the wellbeing of individuals and society. If any laws were to be based on what is contained in any of the three Abrahamic religions of Judaism, Christianity and Islam then the wellbeing of individuals and society will be threatened only on the unproven basis that it is God's commandment and God knows best. Individual sexual preferences between consenting adults will be met by capital punishments of various kinds which include flogging and stoning.[32]   Discrimination between men and women will become acceptable.[33]   Mass murder and genocide of those who are opposed to the established religious idea will be encouraged.[34]   Child sexual abuse will be acceptable.[35]

Furthermore, the idea in many religions that we were created for a specific purpose (for example, in order to attain heaven) usually depends on claims that the information was communicated to us through revelation.   Then an entire argument is constructed on the basis of why

---

[32]Capital punishment of being stoned to death for both the rapist and his victim (because she did not call for help) see: Deuteronomy 22:24; stoning to death for blasphemy see: Leviticus 24:16; stoning to death for idolatry or worshipping other gods see: Deuteronomy 17:2–5, flogging as punishment for crimes see: Deuteronomy 25:1-3; punishment for fornication see: Quran 24:2.

[33]For men being of higher status or ruling over women see: Genesis 3:16; Ephesians 5:22-23; 1 Timothy 2:12; Quran 4:34; for prescription of beating of the wife see: Quran 4:34.

[34]See examples given in previous chapters of this book and footnotes above.

[35]Al-Sayyid Ali al-Sistani, *Minhāj al-ṣālihīn*. v.3, 10, issue 8, accessed on December 15, 2019, https://www.sistani.org/files-new/book-pdf/arabic-menhaj-3.pdf. In his *fatwa* al-Sistani states that intercourse with a girl who a man has married but who has not completed 9 years of age is forbidden but all other types of sexual enjoyment such as touching or feeling with the purpose of enjoyment, erotic kissing and *tafkhidh* (the act of rubbing the penis between the buttocks without insertion) is permitted. Viewing this to be a disturbing edict I proceeded to investigate further and ask other Shia *marāje* (highest ranking legal experts) for their opinion. The responses of most Shia *marāje* regardless of their political affiliation were the same as that of al-Sistani. Note that some of the Shia *marāje* or legal experts of the faith attempted to avert blame by not answering the question of whether other sexual pleasures excluding intercourse with a girl who is under the age of nine is considered permissible by them. However, when the Shia *ūsūlī* (which includes the majority of twelver Shias) system of establishing religious laws are considered it is discovered that those legal experts in reality have confirmed the acceptance of such sexual acts with underage girls. This is because according to the *ūsūlī* Shia legal opinion if a person's *marja* does not give his opinion regarding an issue he or she has the duty to refer to the *marja* who is most knowledgeable after him and who does have an opinion regarding that issue. Hence, in reality those who do not issue an edict forbidding any kind of sexual act with an underage girl are referring their followers to *marja* who does allow it.

revelation is necessary based on the purpose for life given in the revelation itself. This makes the argument for the necessity of revelation a circular argument. Let us say that God did not create in vain and had a purpose for creation. Let us even say that we know that the reason for our creation is to be the best that we can be in terms of intellectual and moral status. Based on the arguments above it would be better to use rational and scientific reasoning to determine the best way we can achieve such a status.

It is reasonable to believe God has given us the ability through rational reasoning and scientific findings to find out for ourselves what is right and wrong. If we were to accept that our mental faculties are not sufficient to understand right and wrong or good and bad then the only other option is not necessarily guidance through revelation.[36] Our rational and scientific understanding of facts, the universe and morality has been developed throughout history through accumulation of knowledge by human beings around the world. If an individual lifespan or mental faculties are not enough there is the entirety of humanity's intellectual capability to consider. Just as we have advanced by sharing our thoughts and knowledge in every field of scientific and philosophical enquiry we can do so regarding what is good and bad.

The second question that needs to be answered by those who claim to have revelation from God is: Why is it that such a guidance is revealed only to a few? The best answer theologians have come up with

---

[36]Ironically the Islamic holy book, the Quran, in chapter 91 (*al-Shams*) verses 7-8 claims that the ability to understand what is good and bad is innate within all human beings.

is that the prophets or those receiving revelation have reached or already are at a certain level of spiritual purity that gives them the capability to receive revelation. Most orthodox interpretations of religions such as Judaism, Christianity and Islam no longer accept new prophets and messengers of God. This means that according to those religious views no other individual can reach that level of spiritual purity anymore. However, no reason is given for why other human beings should not also have the opportunity to purify themselves and receive revelation other than because God has made the decision not to continue sending his guidance that way anymore. The Quran, for example, claims that Muhammad is the final messenger and prophet of God. Islam is supposedly a complete religion that deals with all ethical, moral and legal issues needed by humanity and therefore no need for further revelations. Below I will argue that the Quran and the traditions of Muhammad (in case of Shias the *Ahlul Bayt*) have failed to deal with even everything needed for Islamic practices let alone all the problems of humanity. But also it can be asserted that if we were to reject the claims of the above religions that God has given every human being the ability to purify themselves and receive revelation. Certainly in the view of many including myself, the personalities in Judaism, Christianity and Islam that are asserted to have received revelations from God, either directly or through angels, do not measure up to standards of moral purity according to which many other human beings live their lives.

I would say and many would probably agree that there are and have been many human beings that would find it deplorable to murder an entire ethnic group or people of a nation including children, elderly and livestock on the basis that they had gone away from God's commandments. Joshua, a biblical prophet, on the other hand did not agree and found it justifiable to commit genocide on that basis.[37] There were also other personalities in Judeo-Christian tradition that although not a prophet still were given knowledge of the secrets of God's plan. Take for example the case of Lot who became drunk and committed incest with his daughters.[38] He was supposedly saved from being destroyed along with the rest of the people of Sodom which according to some interpretations were guilty of same sex practices. Angels of God visited Lot and told him of the impending doom and saved him and his daughters.

The personalities in the Christian New Testament do not fare any better when it comes to doing what most people would consider as morally right or refraining from unethical behaviours. Jesus according to many Christian denominations is the son of God or one of the three that comprise the one God. Jesus in the New Testament acts in ways that most people would consider as being immoral and unethical. In one story popularly known as 'Exorcism of the Gerasene demoniac' Jesus orders the demons out of the so called possessed individual to go into swine then proceed to order the swine to drown themselves in a lake. The reason Jesus does so is because the demons begged for him to do so instead of sending them into abyss.[39] Overlooking the complete irrational and unscientific claim made in the story one has no choice but to question the

---

[37]Joshua 6:21.
[38]Genesis 19:30–38.
[39]Mark 5:1-20; Matthew 8:28-34; Luke 8:26-39.

need for sending the demons into the swine rather than just removing them from the possessed individual. A believer in such an irrational story might be tempted to reason that sending the demons into the swine was for the purpose of demonstrating the importance of the life of human beings as opposed to the life of animals. However, such a justification is irrelevant to the criticism. The swine were not killed to feed anybody or even for the enjoyment of taste of its meat. Jesus had other options than, wastefully at best and cruelly in the worst case scenario, to cause the herd of swine to die.[40]

Muhammad attempted to put Judeo-Christian prophets and patriarchs in better light than they are found in the Judaic and Christian scriptures and texts, mostly through omissions of the more violent or scandalous narratives.[41] Lot for example was presented of being a pious prophet and there is no mention of him getting drunk and sleeping with his daughters. Muhammad claimed that corrupt theologians distorted

---

[40]If the story is true that Jesus caused a large number of swine to drown then it was more likely to do with the view of pigs as being impure in the Jewish tradition than any demons. Alternatively it could have been a political act against the food supply of the Romans. The story regarding the demons might have been made up either by Jesus or by the author of the Gospels to justify what had happened. There are indications that the people of the town were not happy about what he had done with their swine herds asking him to leave rather than thanking him. Both Mark and Luke attempt to claim the reason the town's people asked Jesus to leave was out of the fear they had because of the miracle of his exorcism. But if they were just saved from demons it would have more likely that they would thank Jesus than ask him to leave. It seems that they were upset for what he had done with their herds rather than fearful of his supernatural powers.

[41]One reason Muhammad would have wanted to still use the same prophets and personalities found in the Judeo-Christian traditions rather than inventing new ones could have been to attract the followers of those tradition. Another reason could have been that Muhammad himself was a progeny of Abraham and the Judeo-Christian prophets also reflected on his lineage.

scripture that contained factual accounts of his predecessors. However, Muhammad's desire to create better role models does not necessarily mean that the personalities he created were real or acted in the way he described.[42] Muhammad's words regarding the life and character of previous prophets are only accepted to be historically accurate by those who accept the Quran and its narratives to be a revelation from God. Otherwise, there is no reason to reject what has been passed down through other scriptures and historical accounts in favour of Muhammad's version.

Therefore the theologians of Abrahamic religions do not have a good enough reason for their assertion that there is a need for guidance through revelation only to specific people. Even if revelation were to be exclusive to only the pure of spirit then the religious figures in Judaism, Christianity and Islam do not measure up to that standard.

The point could be made that the personalities of the Abrahamic religions should be judged based on the situation during the time period in which they lived in. As I mentioned before many religious figures were reformers and had the intention of improving their society. It could be argued that Muhammad in a society where female infanticide was acceptable, women did not have any inheritance and sons inherited the wives of their fathers (who were not their mothers) was to some degree a woman's rights activist. However, fundamentalist theologians of Abrahamic religions are not claiming their religious personalities to have

---

[42]One might argue that the story of Kaaba being saved by bird hurling rocks from the sky against aggressors was also a better interpretation of Joshua being assisted in his genocide by God hurling huge hailstones on the Canaanites.

been champions of reform only for their time. They claim that their religious personalities are examples to be followed in every era. Furthermore, even if the religious figures did manage to implement a number of beneficial reforms that does not mean that all their ideas were necessarily based on good judgement.

An additional argument can be presented against the idea that only a few chosen individuals with certain level of purity and devotion are chosen by God to deliver His message to humanity. It can be argued that in order to identify the true prophet a person must have an understanding of right and wrong to the level understood by the prophet sent by God. Otherwise it would be impossible for a person who lacks the ability to distinguish between right and wrong to identify a true prophet of God and reject a false prophet. This is because if an ordinary person lacks the capability to know whether or not the action of one claimant to prophethood is right and good while the action of the other is wrong and bad then that person would follow a false prophet without knowing any better. Many religions claim followers of other religions are following false prophets. The only option left is for people to be able to judge as right or wrong the actions of a claimant to prophethood with regards to others and distinguish between a true prophet and a false one. However, if people have the capability to judge between wrong and right then there is no need for the guidance of a prophet or messenger.

It is however important to emphasize that I do not believe there is a need for guidance through revelation of the sort argued for by variety of different religions.[43] I believe our own ability to reason is sufficient for understanding our world, what is right and wrong, and what is good and bad. In fact, I will rationally and scientifically demonstrate the failure of religions to provide sufficient evidence for the claim that their founders or prophets have received revelation from God. Hence the other question that needs to be answered is: Can those claiming to have received guidance or revelation know for certain that such a revelation is from 'the God' rather than other possibilities?

One of the problems with the assertion by someone of having received revelation from God is that they cannot rationally and scientifically prove what they have received is actually from God. In fact, even the person who claims to have received the revelation should not be confident that the revelation is from God. This criticism applies even if it was assumed that the person claiming to have received the revelation (or in some circumstances the inspiration) from God is telling the truth and has not been affected by any kind of psychiatric disorder, drug induced hallucinations or other explanations.

There is simply no rational method that can be applied to prove the current claims of revelation or instructions that had been received by

---

[43]Maybe an argument might be made for receiving inspirations from God which leads to our rational and scientific discoveries as well as inspiring our conscience to identify what is morally right and wrong. But such a supposed method of guidance from God is in no way similar to the autocratic manner revelation based religions require their followers (or in some cases the whole of humanity) to follow a few individuals and theologians who interpret the supposed words of God. There is also the danger of individuals making claims that their inspirations are more superior to others if such a method of guidance becomes authoritative in reasoning for scientific or moral claims.

those who claim to be prophets is from 'the God' rather than numerous other possibilities. I should emphasize that in order to show that one cannot be sure about the source of revelation being from God all that needs to be demonstrated is that there are other possible explanations. The other possible explanations do not have to actually be true. As long as other valid explanations can be given in contrast to the assertion of a revelation being from God then there cannot be certainty with regards to whether it is actually from God. Without certainty one would only follow an assumption. Following assumption is not only irrational and unscientific in the case of claiming revelation from God but also unnecessary especially when it comes to belief about reality and the way we conduct ourselves in our life. In either case, all three religions of Judaism, Christianity and Islam require certainty and conviction from their followers which is not possible if the belief is based on assumptions.

I already indicated that hallucinations or fabrication by a prophet is one possible explanation. After all religions usually attack other religions as having founders that are being deceptive about their claims. But even if those explanations are ruled out another alternative explanation can be given. Suppose that our universe is created by powerful creatures that are also created by something else. They have power over our universe though they themselves are in need of a creator for their world. It is perfectly reasonable to argue that the revelation a particular prophet received was not by 'the God' and creator of everything but by the creator of this universe. The prophet who received the revelation from the creator of this universe would not know any better. One might argue that this other creator who himself needs 'the

God' to exist is not benevolent and therefore instead of guiding humanity sends revelations that are intended to divide and cause conflict between humanity. After all there are many faithful who attack the prophets of other religions and claim the revelation of the other religion is from the devil while their own one is from God.

A case could also be made that such a creator that is limited does not have full knowledge of its creation to know what is right and wrong or good and bad. If we were to create a virtual world or a creature of some kind we too might not have complete knowledge about what we have created. The theologian might be tempted to give a counter argument that 'the God' due to his grace, benevolence and justice would not allow such a creator to treat us that way. If 'the God' allows that, it would go against his grace and benevolence and goodness. In reply, I would argue that in the same way God of theologians allows a king or a ruler to oppress his subjects for purposes of judgement or some sort of greater good then too he can allow this minor creator to carry out his deception or to rule his creation without full knowledge. The God of theologians allows parents to bring up their kids according to beliefs and values they see fit which might be incorrect. In the same way God would allow the minor creator to treat his creation as he wishes without having full knowledge.

A third alternative explanation could be that what the prophet assumed to be revelation from God was actually a being of either an extra-terrestrial origin or of a different form unknown to human beings. Again the prophet who believes he or she has received the revelation would not know any better. I am neither arguing for minor creators or aliens pretending to be God. However, if such alternative answers exist no one can say for certain the revelation is from God and must be obeyed without rational and scientific analysis. Other possible explanations can be given for why someone would wrongly assume they are receiving revelation. For example, it could have been deceptive tactics by other people residing in the area in which a prophet assumed he had received revelation from God. Certain individuals who wanted their desired changes implemented in a society constructed an elaborate plan which included deceiving an individual to think he is a prophet of God receiving revelations.

To believe God has actually communicated with a person a lot of trust must be placed in that person and their ability to be able to identify that which they received as being from God rather than any other source. No personality in any religion has managed to demonstrate such ability if such a demonstration was even possible by them.

The other problem with the claims of having received revelation from God is the numerous erroneous claims that are found in various different scriptures that either oppose scientific findings or seem to indicate lack of knowledge of certain facts. This raises the question: Is there any evidence that can rationally and scientifically demonstrate that the revelations and words of God claimed by a particular religion are in fact not from God? To go through each and every scientific error in different religious scriptures is not the purpose of this text. There is no need to go through each and every error to prove a text cannot be from

God. Other critiques of religious scriptures have already accomplished that task. To show that a religious scripture is not from an omniscient God it only needs to be proven that the text contains at least one error. Even one scientific error in the scripture of a religion proves that the text is not from God. Scholars of religious scriptures might argue that if there are any errors in their religious scripture that is not an indication the entire text is not from God. They can argue that only the part that contains the error is not from God. However, if any error is found in a scripture then there is no possible method that can be used to identify which parts were tainted by human interference and which parts are actually from God. In addition, it needs to be demonstrated that a religious scripture is from God and errors in it create doubt with people asking: Why would God send communication and guidance that is susceptible to interference and distortion?

Among the claims in religious scriptures that are refuted by science is the biblical narrative that the world (or the universe) was created by God in six days, known popularly as the creation story. The creation story is found in one way or another in Judaism, Christianity and Islam. The scientific error in the six day creation story is the way the universe and the Earth is said to have been formed along with the way a day is described. The order which each different part of the universe and Earth is formed and how they were formed does not correspond with scientific findings. There have been attempts by polemics of each religion to interpret the texts of their respective stories to match current scientific findings. But almost any text if ambiguous enough can be interpreted by a person in a way that gives them the meaning they want. If a religious text was from God who intended to demonstrate His knowledge then it would not have been difficult to place points in it that produces a degree of certainty. For example, the Quran talks about the sun and the moon swimming in an orbit.[44]   A 21st Century Muslim might be tempted to interpret the verse in context of modern scientific findings and many have done so. On the basis of modern scientific findings both the Moon is in an orbit around the Earth and the Sun in the Milky Way galaxy. However, Muhammad had no knowledge of modern scientific findings.   What is known from reports of previous exegesis of the Quran and reports from the sayings of Muhammad gives a different explanation for the verse that does not indicate any knowledge of what we now know about the celestial motions. When taken in the context of the understanding of the motions of the moon and the sun in the time and environment of Muhammad the verse only refers to the movement of the Sun and the Moon as he saw it in the sky. Muhammad saw the moon rising from the east and setting in the west supposedly disappearing at the bottom during the night and again coming up from the east. Also during the year depending on the time and season of the year this rising and setting took a different angular motion across the sky.   To the naked eye the movement through the sky looks as if the two objects are "swimming" in the sky. No special knowledge is needed other than what Muhammad had observed like others during his time.

However, what I find the most interesting part of the creation story is the way six days are described. The biblical narrative seems to suggest the entire reality was created in six days after which God having

---

[44]Quran 21:33.

been exhausted rested on the seventh day.[45] One could enquire about the reason why God who is not bound by physical laws and who created them would be exhausted by creating the universe.[46] It seems the biblical narrative assumed God like other creatures is bound by the laws of nature and not its creator. Such a claim raises the issue that the biblical God is not a God at all and following his commandments is not necessary. For the purpose of this argument however I will limit myself to demonstrating the erroneous ways theologians of the above mentioned religions have attempted to justify the primitive way that their religious texts talk about day and night. This can then demonstrate that the words attributed to God cannot be from the creator of the universe. The creator of the universe would certainly know the cause of day and night on Earth.

The biblical narrative seems to suggest that the universe or at least the Earth was literally created in six days. This is absolutely false from what we now know from scientific findings about the history of the universe. Muhammad seems to have understood that the claim that the world was actually created in six days is absurd. Hence, in the Quran we find passages that claim a day with 'Allah' (the term used in Islam for God)

---

[45]Genesis 1: 1-31 and Genesis 2: 1-3.

[46]Attempts have been made to interpret the text as meaning that God ceased his creation rather than rest. First, the texts seem to clearly indicate that God needed a rest due to having created so much. Second, such an explanation means that God, like the carpenter mentioned before, is only a cause for the universe's design but not its continued existence. But as explained before an existential cause that has brought something into existence *ex nihilo* (out of nothing) needs to continue to maintain its existence otherwise it would need something else to maintain its existence. If something else could maintain its existence then there was no need for God as its existential cause to begin with.

is like a thousand or fifty thousand Earthly years.[47] But Muhammad's version is not any more scientifically accurate than that of the biblical narrative. Furthermore, the calculation of the number of night and day requires the universe and the Earth to have already been created. Such a calculation requires Earth's rotation about its own axis and the existence of the Sun to create the day. This is necessary even with a geocentric view of the universe.

Those who attempt to defend the scriptures that contain the idea of six day creationism can always argue that six days in the scriptures is not the literal six days. As mentioned above theologians can argue that the meaning of the word day should not be taken literally.[48] If taken metaphorically the meaning of the text that God created the universe in six days is intended to demonstrate the power of God rather than give a scientific calculation of the period of time it took for universe to come into existence. Muslim theologians can further argue that the discrepancy between a day with God being equivalent to a thousand in some verses and fifty thousand in other verses proves the metaphoric usage of the word 'day'. Such arguments however do not taken into account the rational consequences of interpreting the term 'day' in a different way to its actual meaning. There does not seem to be any reason why a revelation or scripture from God would go through the trouble of giving an exact number for how long it took God to create the universe only to want the reader to interpret it metaphorically. In the case of the Quran, it

---

[47]Quran 22:47, 32:5, 70:4.

[48]Although the Bible is quite clear that there was a morning and an evening to make one day.

seems absolutely unnecessary for God to first say He created the universe in six days only to be ambiguous about what a day means. Furthermore, a day with God would be different to that of Earth only if God inhabited a world with its own night and day cycles. The message of God's power in regards to the creation of the universe would have been better expressed if God had said that since He is not limited by time he created the universe in an instance. Quran even claims that when God wants to create something He only needs to say, "Be" and it is.[49] But for some reason Muhammad decided to keep the idea of the universe being created in six days. He probably did so because he wanted to keep the Judeo-Christian tradition that he claimed to have preceded him but predicted his coming.

There are also clear indications in the scriptures of the different religions of the lack of understanding of their author of certain facts. This lack of knowledge can be explained as being due to what was known and not known at the time of the author, especially in his community. Take for example the Islamic prescriptions for the daily obligatory prayers and the practice of fasting during the month of Ramadan. Both the obligatory daily prayers (*salāt*) and fasting or abstinence (*sawm*) of the month of Ramadan is seen by most Islamic sects as being of the most important pillars of the religion of Islam. There are clear times allocated for prayers based on the rising and setting of the sun. There are also clear instructions (with minor differences between sects) regarding the abstinence of the month of Ramadan based on the daily apparent motion

---

[49]Quran 36:82.

of the sun. Hence, there are rules about when to abstain from eating and certain other activities at dawn and when to be released from such abstinence at sunset. The prayer and fasting times given in the Quran and religious narratives close to the time of Muhammad (including those instructions given by the Shia Imams) consider only the day and night cycle found between certain geographical location. There is no mention of how one should observe prayer and fasting in areas where a day or a night can last many months such as the north and south poles or cities close to them. The texts are completely silent when it comes to observing such rituals outside of Earth or on other planets.

The problem for Islam is that it claims to be the perfect religion that includes in it everything needed for humanity until the end of time. However, if it fails to give divine guidance on how to perform obligatory prayers or conduct fasting rituals of Ramadan in certain geographical locations on Earth or any place outside of Earth then it is not complete even in regards to its own fundamental pillars. If Islam fails to adequately guide its followers with regards to its most fundamental pillars then it fails to prove it is a complete religion for every need of humanity.

The reason there are no instructions in the original sources of Islam (Quran and Sunnah for the Sunnis or Quran and the traditions of the *Ahlul Bayt* for the Shias) in regard to daily prayer and abstinence of Ramadan outside of Earth and in the polar regions of Earth is the lack of knowledge of its founder regarding certain facts. Muhammad and many of the early Muslim holy figures that followed were not aware of the science behind the day and night cycles on Earth. In fact, they had no knowledge of the North Pole and the South Pole and probably assumed night and day occurs in the same way across the visible universe (a geocentric view of the universe).[50] Muslim theologians that came after the scientific discoveries that provided humanity with everything needed for an accurate account of the night and day cycles and celestial motions were then able to give *fatwas* (religious edicts) of how obligatory prayer and abstinence in Ramadan should be performed in the polar poles or outside of Earth.[51] Their edicts however do not excuse the fact that the original source was not adequate and the original founder of the religion lacked the understanding that was needed for him to provide the guidance himself.

The final question that needs to be assessed is: What proof or evidence do individuals claiming to have received the word or guidance of God have for their claim? The 'evidence' used by almost all religions as proof for the divinity of their claims is the occurrences of miracles. Miracles are supposed to demonstrate the connection of the holy figure to the divine through their ability to manipulate physical laws of the universe. The argument is that everything in the physical universe is bound by its laws. If an individual is capable of manipulating or altering the physical laws of the universe then that person must have a connection to the source and creator of those laws. Only the source and creator of

---

[50]Hence, for example, they probably assumed during the day the entire visible universe is lit.

[51]Islamic theologians have now formulated instructions on how to observe obligatory daily prayers and fasting during the month of Ramadan in the circumstances mentioned above. However, the point still remains that such prescriptions did not come from God but people themselves only after such places were made known to theologians.

the laws of the universe is capable of changing or manipulating them. Therefore, the one who is sent by the creator, that is to say God, can alter and manipulate the laws of the universe through the power given to him by that creator. Hence, according to the Abrahamic religious narratives Moses can part the sea by the power given to him by God. Jesus can cure the blind because of either being a god himself (dominant Christian view) or been given the power to do so by God (Islamic view) and so forth. Even today many believe in miraculous events that are due to some kind of connection either directly to God or through a holy figure. The Catholic Church canonizes a person as a saint based on the number of miracles performed by them.

The idea that miracles prove the connection to the divine can face two main challenges. The first challenge is providing evidence that a miracle actually took place. All claims of historical miracles contained in the various different religious traditions in existence today lack any rational and scientific evidence for their veracity. Simply being mentioned in a text that a miracle took place is not sufficient reason for it to have happened. Even if such an event thought to be miraculous at the time did happen, a proper critical analysis needs to take place before it can be verified as being an actual miracle. Most claims of historical miracles, such as the parting of the sea by Moses or the curing of the blind by Jesus, is impossible to be examined critically thousands of years after its purported occurrence. We now know many stories contained in the Judeo-Christian traditions and Islam can in fact be traced back to mythologies that preceded them.

Claims of miracles at present however can be critically examined and after thorough investigation no evidence for their existence has been provided to date that can withstand a critical rational and scientific analysis.

Even if it were to be accepted that such events as parting of the sea or the curing of the blind did take place it does not prove a connection to a divine creator. In both situations the event can still take place if the technology for it existed. The events do not technically go against the natural laws of the physical universe. Using the same argument used to deny verification of claims of revelations from God it can be argued that such 'miracles' could actually not be from God. There is the possibility that a more powerful being (say a creator of this world who also was created by another creator more powerful than him) or beings more advanced in technology (extra-terrestrials) could have assisted Jesus, Moses or any other Prophets. I am not claiming that such beings did in fact assist either Moses or Jesus since I do not believe the veracity of the stories of the miraculous events. However if other possible explanations can be given for why such phenomena, if true, did occur it is sufficient to show absence of or connection to divinity.

Muslims claim two different types of miracles for Muhammad. One type of miracle is similar to that of other Judeo-Christian tradition in the sense that Muhammad is said to have altered and manipulated the physical laws of the universe. One example mentioned in the Quran is the parting of the moon.[52] Muhammad is said to have split the moon into

---

[52]Quran 54:1-2

two as a sign of his prophethood. He is said to have asked each denier to observe how he is able to split and then put back together the moon. After the supposed miracle the Quran states that the deniers did not believe him and called his actions sorcery or magic. Considering that his miracle did not convince those who were present during his time it would be even more difficult for anyone to accept it now without any evidence other than Muslim believers who are convinced of the veracity of the Quran and the traditions passed down verbally. However, such faithful conviction has nothing to do with rational and scientific evidence.[53]

The second type of miracle that Muhammad is said to have brought as proof of his claim to have received revelation from God is the Islamic scripture itself known as the Quran. Almost all Muslim sects consider Quran to be the living miracle of Muhammad which proves his prophethood and messengership from God. The miracle of the Quran is supposed to be literary. However, Muslims scholars and theologians have had difficulty trying to prove what exactly the literary miracle of the Quran is. Some have claimed the beauty of its verses.[54] Others have claimed that the Quran is comprehensive in its content. There have also

---

[53]Interestingly, Shia theologians make an argument for why Muhammad in order to prove his prophethood did not produce the kind of miracles that was requested from him by his deniers. The reason they give is that if he did produce the miracles they requested it would without doubt prove his prophethood. If his prophethood was proven without doubt and the deniers continued not to believe in him it would lead to their immediate destruction through a punishment sent by God as was the case with previous prophets of God. However, this Quranic narrative of the splitting of the moon proves that immediate destruction does not follow the deniers of Muhammad's Prophethood after he performs a clear miracle.

[54]It should be kept in mind that the current order of the Quran is not in the chronological order it was revealed. Hence, each verse is usually analysed independently by Islamic scholars.

been attempts to show that the Quran either predicted future events or stated scientific truth that was impossible to know at the time. In terms of the purported scientific facts and predictions of future events as mentioned above is only based on arbitrary interpretation of general and ambiguous verses. I have already demonstrated that the Quran is not comprehensive in its content regarding some of its most fundamental prescriptions. This lack of comprehensiveness is not improved when the traditions of Muhammad (and *Ahlul Bayt* in general for Shias) is taken into consideration.

The purported claim of the beauty of the verses of the Quran is even more arbitrary than the other reasons as proof for it being miraculous. There is no adequate guideline or criteria produced by any Islamic scholar that has managed to objectively demonstrate the literary beauty of the Quranic miracle. Furthermore, if Quran's miracle is its literary beauty in the Arabic language it is not much use for convincing those who do not speak or understand Arabic. Expecting people to learn an entire language and its literary intricacies to understand a miracle is an irrational expectation for producing conviction of a miracle. The other alternative of trusting a Muslim theologian who does understand the Arabic language is absurd especially since there are different sects with their own views and ethical and moral conducts in Islam. This raises the question that a person could theoretically follow a "misguided" sect.

In conclusion, the religion of Islam fails to prove any miracles for Muhammad just as Christianity fail to prove for Jesus and Judaism fails to prove for the Jewish prophets.

4   Hinduism

There are currently two other influential religions with a large number of followers that are not from the traditions of Abrahamic religions. One of those religions is the pantheon of Hinduism. Hinduism is not technically one single religion. Hinduism is used to refer to a multitude of beliefs that have originated in the Indian subcontinent. All those beliefs share some common traditions and hence identify with the term Hindu. The term itself used as a reference to a religion is European construct in order to distinguish it as a single religion from other religions.[55] Originally it came from the Persian term that referred to the people who lived beyond the river Indus without mention of their religious beliefs. Most of the people who others refer to as Hindus usually identify themselves based on the region they come from, for example Gujaratis (people who come from the region of Gujarat), the deity they worship (also termed currents), for example Shaivism or Shaktism and other deities, or the caste they belong to, for example Soni (goldsmiths). Due to the fact that Hinduism has no

---

[55]Wendy Doniger, *On Hinduism*, New York: Oxford University Press, 2014, 3-9.

unified canon as such and is comprised of different belief systems it cannot be analysed as one religious doctrine. The main criticism that can apply to the pantheon of Hinduism is that like other religious traditions there is no rational and scientific evidence to prove many of its claims found in the belief system of its currents.   The philosophical ideas regarding life after death through reincarnation, the creation mythologies found in its currents, the theory of Karma (an idea it shares with Buddhism) and many other religious concepts found in the pantheon of Hinduism are clearly derived from ancient mythologies and are not backed by modern scientific findings.

However, one of the most crucial criticisms of the Hindu pantheon is issues found in the tradition that promotes injustice, inequality and unjustifiable discrimination. The roots of these issues can be traced back to the superstitious beliefs contained in the tradition used to justify the injustice, inequality and discrimination. Among such issues is the caste system which is not only prevalent in India but also among Hindus outside of India. Caste system is a rigid hierarchical system that divides every individual into different social and occupational classes from birth. A person's caste decides their occupation, status in society, who they can marry, how they can act in certain circumstances and even whether or not they can touch or interact with people of different castes. The Hindu scriptures Mahabharata and Bhagavad Gita have justified the caste system by stating that every individual has in their nature certain qualities and abilities that place them in a particular societal group.[56]

---

[56]See for example: Bhagavad Gita 18: 40-47.

The belief in the idea among Hindus that those of Indian ethnicity must fall under one of the castes pervades even among many traditional Hindus outside of India. Marriages are usually arranged between a man and a woman of the same caste and inter-caste marriages are opposed by more traditional Hindu parents. The caste system has led to discrimination and violence which many people face in India where Hinduism is the majority religion. Discrimination based on the caste system has and continues to lead to social inequality and violence against those who go against the tradition and practices associated with it in India. Discriminations based on the caste system includes limitations in job and career paths of individuals and their social status including how they are treated by law enforcement or government agencies. Violence is regularly committed against those who do not accept their social status or who marry outside of their caste especially if the marriage is to a person considered to be of a higher caste.[57]

Another discriminatory practice found among the Hindu pantheon traditions is the treatment of women. The practice of Chaupadi for

---

[57]For examples of social inequality with regards to the caste system see: Michael Saafi, "'I'm born to do this': Condemned by caste, India's sewer cleaners risk death daily," *The Guardian*, March 04, 2018, https://www.theguardian.com/world/2018/mar/04/im-born-to-do-this-condemned-by-caste-indias-sewer-cleaners-risk-death-daily; for examples of violent reaction to those who marry outside of the caste see: Canada: Immigration and Refugee Board of Canada, "India: Situation of inter-caste couples, particularly those involving Dalits, from both urban and rural locations, including societal attitudes, treatment by government authorities and the treatment of their children (2005-April 2012)," *Refworld*, May 11, 2012, https://www.refworld.org/docid/50b49e872.html; for an examples of the type of violence associated with the caste system see: Vineet Khare, "The Indian Dalit man killed for eating in front of upper-caste men," *British Broadcasting Corporation*, May 20, 2019, https://www.bbc.com/news/world-asia-india-48265387.

example, which is more prominent among Hindus in Nepal and South India, considers women to be impure during their menstrual cycle. Their impurity is considered a bad omen that could affect family, livestock and even be disrespectful to certain deities. Hence, at the extreme end menstruating women are told to stay away from the house until the end of their menstruation. A more moderate practice requires the menstruating woman to stay in a different room while food is passed to her with a long stick or in some other way.[58]

The Hindu theological and legal texts also encourage the subservience of women to men. The following passage can be found about a women's position in regards to men in the Manusmṛiti:

2. Day and night women must be kept in dependence by the males (of) their (families), and, if they attach themselves to sensual enjoyments, they must be kept under one's control.

---

[58]For an example of the practice of isolating menstruating women see: Sarah Stacke, "The Risky Lives of Women Sent Into Exile—For Menstruating," National Geographic, March 10, 2017, https://www.nationalgeographic.com/photography/proof/2017/03/menstruation-rituals-nepal/; "Nepal woman and children die in banned 'menstruation hut'," British Broadcasting Corporation, January 10, 2019, https://www.bbc.com/news/world-asia-46823289; also see: Megha Mohan, "'I couldn't mourn my grandmother because I had my period'," British Broadcasting Corporation, February 12, 2018, https://www.bbc.com/news/stories-42608302; Hannah Sparks, "Women form 385-mile human wall to protest period shaming," New York Post, January 3, 2019, https://nypost.com/2019/01/03/women-form-385-mile-human-wall-to-protest-period-shaming/; Rupa Jha, "100 Women 2014: The taboo of menstruating in India," British Broadcasting Corporation, October 27, 2014, https://www.bbc.com/news/world-asia-29727875.

3. Her father protects (her) in childhood, her husband protects (her) in youth, and her sons protect (her) in old age; a woman is never fit for independence.[59]

Such passages indicate that keeping women in a subservient position to that of a man and controlling her behaviour is encouraged and advised in the Hindu religious traditions. No rational reason is given, as is usually the case when making such laws, for why the woman needs to be kept under the control of the man.

As a general rule as it has been emphasized throughout this book the Kashfence Philosophy rejects the imposition of any belief and practice that is not rooted in rational and scientific analysis. Hence, if a belief or practice is not proven through rational and scientific means it is rejected and it does not matter to a Kashfenci whether its source is from a monotheistic religion, a polytheistic religion or not based in any religion.

Hence according to the Kashfenci philosophical view there should be no discrimination based on gender, race or other such irrational criteria.

---

[59]*The Laws of Manu*, edited by G. Buhler, Oxford: The Clarendon Press, 1886, 327-8.

5   Geographical Limitations of Religions

The major religions practiced today can be divided into religions that claim to have been sent by God to all humanity and religions that are or were at one time limited to a particular ethnic group. In both cases the religion's advent was limited to a particular geographical location and was influenced by the environment it came from and the cultures familiar to its founders. The divine origins of a religion can be questioned on the basis that a religion was influenced by the limits of the environment it came from or the cultures its founders was familiar with. A religion sent or revealed by the creator of the universe, even if that creator is not 'the God', with the purpose of being a universal guiding force for humanity should include directives and guidance that takes into account and satisfies the need of every human culture and environment. Therefore, if a religious scripture and its ideas and instructions are limited by the environment and cultures of its founder then there is no divine origin.

The Hindu pantheon for example originated from the Indian subcontinent. Traditionally, ethnic groups within the Indian subcontinent worshipped deities that originated from that particular group's mythology. Efforts were not made to promulgate their religious thoughts to others outside of their immediate community, tribe or ethnic group. Only in the recent time period have the so called spiritual masters who have come from the traditions of the Hindu pantheon have attempted to propagate and have accepted converts outside of their immediate ethnic groups. In case of the Hindu pantheon, its rigid caste and hierarchal systems found in many of its versions makes conversion in most cases difficult if not impossible. The Hindu *Itihasa* (history) which includes Mahabharata, the Ramayana, and Puranas include mythologies which is almost exclusively limited to the Indian subcontinent and which probably had their origins in the over exaggerations and alterations of historical events. Puranas could be interpreted to include a wider cosmological view not limited to the Indian subcontinent but is nevertheless contextually limited to the deities and mythologies practiced in that region.

Judaism is mostly limited to a particular ethnic group, namely the Children of Israel, as conversion is a very difficult and complicated process and does not happen often. The religious corpus of Judaism is mainly an expression of the traditions of the Jewish people and their supposed covenant with God. Most prophets and figures of prominence in Judaic religious scriptures are of Jewish ethnicity and concentration is mainly on the history of the Jewish people. There have been many studies conducted on the origins of the stories and accounts in the Jewish religious and historical texts. For example, the idea of the great flood during the time of Noah has already been traced to a similar story in the Epic of Gilgamesh. The same stories in the Christian and Islamic scriptures were also taken from the Jewish tradition. Hence, I do not see a need to further analyse the stories contained in the Jewish tradition in this work as it has already been done in various different works.

Current religions with significant number of adherents that claim to have brought a universal message to all humanity are Christianity and Islam. Both religions do no limit themselves to a particular region or ethnic group and aim to spread the word they claim to be from God among humanity. Similar to Hinduism and Judaism the origins and scriptures of Christianity and Islam are limited in their religious beliefs and ritual practices based on the influences of the geographical location, time period and the cultures familiar to their founders and developers. For example, traditionally Christianity came from the Jewish tradition incorporating many of its teachings into their own theology. It can also be argued that Egyptian, Roman and Greek traditions also influenced Christianity especially with regards to later denominations such as the Roman Catholic Church.

Muhammad too integrated the biblical stories of the Judeo-Christian traditions into the Quran. Interestingly Muhammad did not limit himself to what he found in the bible. For example, the Islamic description of the process of what happens to the spirit of a person after death is taken from the Zoroastrian eschatology. In Zoroastrianism after death a person has to cross a bridge into the afterlife known as the Chinvat Bridge or the Činwad Puhl. The appearance of the Chinvat Bridge is either narrow or wide depending on a person's righteousness. If the person has been righteous the bridge will appear wide and that person can pass without trouble. However, if the person was wicked the bridge will appear narrow and that person will be dragged to a place of eternal punishment.[60] Similarly, in Islam a person will pass a bridge known as *sirāt* when passing into the afterlife. This bridge is either narrow making it difficult to pass if the person was not pious or wide making it easy to pass if the person was pious. The issue of Islamic practices due to the limited knowledge of its founder about celestial movements was already discussed in chapter three.

The other issue that questions the universality of religions like Christianity and Islam is that such a claim does not correlate with their account of God's retribution of the unbelievers. According to both Christianity and Islam acceptance of their religion as the true religion and its main tenets is essential for a person to enter heaven (a blissful and enjoyable place reserved for the pious to live in for eternity). But there were groups of people who did not have contact with the founders of Christianity and Islam or the later propagators of either religion until a long period of time after their advent. For example, Native Americans were not in contact with much of the world until the first contact with Europeans in the 15th and 16th century C.E. The only conclusion would be that these groups who did not accept the religion of Christianity and Islam due to being unaware of them were condemned by God to enter hell (a place of suffering reserved for the unbelievers and the wicked). A god who does not send a message to a community but condemns them to hell

---

[60]Aḥmad Tafażżolī, *Encyclopaedia Iranica, Online Edition*, s.v. "Činwad Puhl," December 15, 1991, Vol. V, Fasc. 6, 594-5, http://www.iranicaonline.org/articles/cinwad-puhl-av.

is unjust which is in contradiction to the attribute of justice claimed for God in both the Christian and the Islamic traditions.

Theologians from the two religious traditions have argued that anyone who has not received the message of Christ, in terms of Christianity or the message of Allah, in terms of Islam, is not condemned until the time which they are made aware of God's guidance. This justification however leads to an essential problem. A person who is condemned to hell by God for not following a particular religion after he was introduced to it could make an argument for the injustice of the Christian or Islamic God. She could argue that if a Native American person who did not yet have contact with the true religion was not required to follow it and avoid going to hell and maybe even enter heaven then why was not the same courtesy extended to her instead of introducing her to religion. If God answers that she could have had a higher status than the Native American if she had passed the test set out for her and accepted the true religion then the Native American person can argue why such an opportunity was not given to him.

The fact of the matter is that the founders of Christianity and Islam and subsequent polemics and theologians of its traditions could not correlate their concept of a just God that metes out reward and punishment through heaven and hell with the realities of the world, its inhabitants and geographical limitations.

6 The Kashfence Philosophy

The word Kashfence is made up of two words 'kashf' which in some languages means to discover and the suffix '-ence' which means denoting a quality or an action or its result. Together 'kashf' and 'ence' create the original word Kashfence intended to capture the essence of discovering through rational and scientific reasoning and analysis. The Kashfence philosophy is comprised of the following five principles:

1 - Rational and Scientific reasoning

2 - There is one unlimited God

3 - Justice

4 - Family

5 - Healthy Mind and Body

<u>Rational and Scientific reasoning</u>

Knowledge can be attained through rational and scientific reasoning only. Every person of sound mind has the ability to think and reason for themselves   as individuals and as a group assisting each other. Reasoning, as long as it is on the basis of rational and scientific analysis is what leads to discovery of truth and reality. Kashfence philosophy puts the most emphasis on this principle and all other principles are subject to proof and evidence through rational and scientific reasoning.

God

In accordance with Kashfence philosophy God is not limited in any shape or form, is the existential cause of everything and the laws that govern their interaction but does not have an existential cause itself (has always existed) and cannot be divided in any way. No person or limited being can claim to be god or divine.

Justice

There exists a sense of justice within people. Rational and scientific reasoning, not claims of divine laws, should be used to clarify what is just and fair.

Family

Whatever form a family takes it is beneficial to be caring to one's family and socialise with them and protect them.

Healthy Mind and Body

To enjoy life and help others enjoy life, a healthy mind and body is essential. Hence, in order to achieve the aforementioned goal every individual should endeavour to the best of their ability to have a healthy mind and body and help others to do the same.

The Kashfenci philosophy is intended to provide every individual with a philosophy of life free from superstition that can assist a person to live life in the best way possible for them. It encourages critical thinking based on rational and scientific evidence not based on claims of divine commandments. In this way, the Kashfence philosophy leaves room for people to figure out and customise their life in accordance to what they think is best for them. However, being good and accepting the rights of others and establishing justice are all goals of a Kashfenci. According to the Kashfenci philosophical view having beliefs which do not correspond with reality and is based on superstitious reasoning would be damaging to a person's mind and body and also to the society at large. On an individual level it is based on the idea that every individual seeks to know what is true even if there are social and psychological reasons for them to pretend or act according to superstitious beliefs. A person's desire to know the truth creates a conflict within that person if they were to pretend or act according to something which they know not to be true. If, however, they were to truly believe in a false claim then that false claim could have a damaging effect on their mind and body in many different ways.

For example, many religions have religious laws that encourage, discourage or outright forbid their followers from certain acts. These acts could include prevention of actions that cause harm to others. In such cases the Kashfenci way of thinking would agree with them that if such actions are proven through evidence to be harmful and unjust to others or takes away the rights of others then a person has a responsibility to prevent themselves from such actions. Murder, rape and theft are examples of actions that a person has a responsibility to prevent. Society too should create laws to prevent such harms and injustices.

On the other hand, there are many religious instructions and laws that prevent people from certain habits and actions or instruct them to act in a certain way for which there is no evidence of harm or injustice and is simply the view of the creator of the religion or its followers. It could have been the case that the prevention of such habits and actions or instructions for a particular practice might have been beneficial for a certain cultural environment or for a certain geographical location. But the same benefit cannot apply in other geographical locations or other cultural environments. In fact, it might be better to change the cultural environment so that the same restrictions and instructions no longer need to be applied. Examples of religious prohibitions which do not seem to be backed by evidence but is rather the preference of the founders of the religions are laws to do with consumption of food and sexual activity. Similarly, some obligatory acts in religions are for the purpose of fulfilling the ideas of the founders of a religion or creating a society based on the principles believed by those founders to be true.

Kashfence philosophy is not against obligations and prohibitions of religions simply because they are of a particular religion. In fact, if rational and scientific evidence is provided for why people should refrain from an action or observe an action then the follower of Kashfenci philosophy would accept it. The problem occurs when the obligations and prohibitions are claimed to be good based on the claim that they are from God or based on beliefs assumed to be true by a religion devoid of rational and scientific evidence. Since according to the Kashfence Philosophy no direct revelation or commandment has been sent from God and no one has been chosen to deliver God's message such claims are fully rejected. Only claims backed by rational and scientific evidence is acceptable.

In fact, as it was discussed above, many religions were probably started by individuals that believed and desired for reform in their society. Prohibitions such as the ones that intended to stop the killing of the innocent people are something that has rational evidence for it. However, for example, the idea of sex outside of a specific marriage ceremony lacks evidence for having anything to do with justice. It seems religious laws regarding sexual activities is a way of controlling individual's freedom when it comes to sex, giving control of the sexual activities of one gender over to another, or advocating for a sexual preference over other preferences. Religions with such restrictions usually do not provide rational and scientific evidence other than God's commandment for why such laws are in place. On that basis, the reason the adherent of that religion restrict themselves from doing what is prohibited is the covenant they make with God not to act against what they believe to be the commandment or word of God. However, as it was demonstrated no one has managed to rationally and scientifically prove having actually received the commandment or word of God. On that basis, restricting one's self without rational and scientific evidence is unnecessary and at best is missing out on something that can enhance life's enjoyment and at worst harmful to both the self and others.

Some theologians and apologetics of different religions have attempted to bring 'proof' and 'evidence' for why a certain action is made obligatory or prohibited in their religion. Such proofs usually assume the truth of many underlying premises made in that religion. Furthermore, at best without evidence for direct commandment from God such proofs and evidence in many circumstances can only demonstrate the act is good to do or not to do rather than one must not or must do it.[61]

There is the inner drive within every individual to know the truth. The intensity of the desire to know the truth is so much so that it instigates us to not only seek the truth but to also propagate that truth to others. Regardless of the philosophical thought a person comes from, whether that is religious, atheistic or something else the innumerable individuals propagating their thoughts to others is a demonstration of people's desire to accept and spread what they believe to be the truth. Furthermore, with most people there seems to be a desire within the self to do what is good and establish justice. In other words, whether it is for the desire to have a good functioning society, enhancing our life experiences together, or simply living in a safe environment most people seem to desire a moral code of conduct for interacting with each other. Others, and I am included in that group, believe there is an inner desire to

---

[61]If adherents of a religion want to demonstrate why on an individual or societal level certain actions should be prohibited or obligatory then they must through rational and scientific proof and evidence show that to be the case. This must be done without making assumptions about the truth of their religious teachings as the basis for their reasoning.

be moral and good. Kashfence philosophy attempts to make such inner drives and desires into a way of thinking and by extension a way of life.

In Kashfence philosophy an individual makes a promise to God, one's self and others. That promise is to first and foremost believe and make claims about what is outside of the mind on the basis of rational and scientific evidence. Second, the individual makes a promise to God, one's self and others to be good and just in one's life based, once again, on what can be rationally and scientifically proven to be good and just.

According to the Kashfenci way of thinking one makes a voluntary promise to adhere to the aforementioned principles. However, unlike the requirements of many religions discussed above the promise (which in theological terms is termed a covenant) of a Kashfenci should not be based on assumptions that lack rational and scientific evidence. In the Kashfence Philosophy a claim is not made that there are individuals that have direct contact with God who has given them instructions on what should or should not be done or believe. It is up to individuals themselves and with collaboration with others to figure out how they want to live and interact with each other making rational and scientific evidence as their guide.

An objection might be raised against the Kashfenci philosophical view by stating that the domain of science is the physical world whereas as morality is not a physical thing to be analysed scientifically. However, accepting that morality is not something that can be found in the physical world does not eliminate the possibility of the role of science in proving morality. Issues with which scientific findings can assist in making a moral decision can include but is not limited to the identifying factors that shows a person is a conscious human being for the purposes of abortion or other medical conditions that require life support. Another example is that scientific reasoning can be used to counter arguments used by racial supremacists by demonstrating that there is no scientific reason for categorising different ethnic groups based on their appearance or discriminating based on ethnicity. Furthermore, the Kashfence Philosophy expounds the idea that everything requires scientific but also rational proof. Hence, justice and moral principles can be established through rational analysis using scientific evidence.

On an individual level personal preferences should be decided by individuals themselves or between individuals if it involves more than one person. For example, according to the Kashfence Philosophy the structure of the family is not restricted to a particular type. Individuals can decide for themselves and between each other about what constitutes a family. What is important to understand is that people need to take care of each other and this starts with the family.

To have an enjoyable life it is vital to be healthy. Health is both in regards to our body and our mind.   According to the Kashfenci philosophical view rational and scientific evidence should be used to discover what is best for the physical and mental wellbeing of every individual. Every individual should endeavour to be the best they can be physically and mentally in a way that is healthy and enjoyable for them. The community also has a responsibility to assist its members to be healthy physically and mentally.

For a community to be cohesive there needs to be some shared practices and a method of getting together for the purpose of exchanging ideas and socialising with one another. The development of Kashfence philosophy was purposefully intended to not restrict individual preferences and likes other than what is rationally and scientifically proven to be against justice. Individual freedom is a very important concept of Kashfence Philosophy. Hence, laws and practices of a community who live by Kashfenci philosophical doctrine are decided through secular rational and scientific analysis and avoidance of superstition and are subject to evolve and change. Peaceful existence and sanctity of life and to be free from harm should be important for every Kashfenci as any rational moral view would consider such principles to be fundamental to justice and the wellbeing of the individual and society.

Human societies have many events of significance that are either celebrated or commemorated as a yearly anniversary. Such events might have religious, national or ethnic significance or a combination of one or more things. In order to adhere to the secular nature of the Kashfenci philosophical doctrine two days of celebration have been established to celebrate and commemorate what can be universally accepted as being fundamental to happiness and a moral life. Hence, the Kashfence Philosophical doctrine has two days of celebration during the year. One is on 1st of May known as Good Deeds Day on which a Kashfenci does a good deed usually for someone else. The second is on 1st of November known as Family and Friends Day intended to be a day you spend with your family and/or friends.

It is important to also have a place for gathering for the purpose of exchanging ideas and socialising. In keeping with the essence of the word *kashf* which means to discover (in the context of the Kashfence Philosophy through rational and scientific analysis) the Kashfenci community will have communal gatherings in what is known as the Discovery Centres. At such centres people engage in discussions, listen to lectures and have the opportunity to socialize.

With the expounding of the Kashfence Philosophy in the final chapter of this book I have completed the basis for the Kashfence Philosophy, the philosophy of discovering truth only through rational and scientific reasoning.

Bibliography

Al-Hilli, Hasan b. Yusuf b.'Ali Ibnu'l-Mutahhar. *Al-Bābu 'l-Hādī 'Ashar (A Treatise on the Principles of Shi'ite Theology.* London: The Royal Asiatic Society, 1928.

Al-Sistani, Al-Sayyid Ali. *Minhāj al-ṣālihīn.* Accessed on December 15, 2019, https://www.sistani.org/files-new/book-pdf/arabic-menhaj-3.pdf

Canada: Immigration and Refugee Board of Canada. "India: Situation of inter-caste couples, particularly those involving Dalits, from both urban and rural locations, including societal attitudes, treatment by government authorities and the treatment of their children (2005-April 2012)." *Refworld*, May 11, 2012, https://www.refworld.org/docid/50b49e872.html.

Casullo, Albert. "A Priori Knowledge." In *The Oxford Handbook of Epistemology.* Edited by Paul K. Moser. New York: Oxford University Press, 2002.

Goldstein, Laurence. "The Barber, Russell's Paradox, and More." In *The Law of Non-Contradiction: New Philosophical Essays*, ed. Graham Priest, J.C. Beall, and Bradley Armour-Garb. New York: Oxford University Press, 2004.

Hannah Sparks. "Women form 385-mile human wall to protest period shaming." *New York Post*, January 3, 2019, https://nypost.com/2019/01/03/women-form-385-mile-human-wall-to-protest-period-shaming/.

Jha, Rupa. "100 Women 2014: The taboo of menstruating in India." *British Broadcasting Corporation*, October 27, 2014, https://www.bbc.com/news/world-asia-29727875.

Khare, Vineet. "The Indian Dalit man killed for eating in front of upper-caste men." *British Broadcasting Corporation*, May 20, 2019, https://www.bbc.com/news/world-asia-india-48265387.

Khorasani, Wahid. *Tozīh al-Masā`el* . Qom: Madrese Bāqer al-'Ulūm, 1381 H.S.

Kroon, Frederick. "Realism and Dialetheism." In *The Law of Non-Contradiction: New Philosophical Essays*, ed. Graham Priest, J.C. Beall, and Bradley Armour-Garb. New York: Oxford University Press, 2004.

MacGirk, Tim. "Hindu world divided by a 24-hour wonder." *Independent*, September 23, 1995, https://www.independent.co.uk/news/uk/hindu-world-divided-by-a-24-hour-wonder-1602382.html.

Mohan, Megha. "'I couldn't mourn my grandmother because I had my period'." *British Broadcasting Corporation*, February 12, 2018, https://www.bbc.com/news/stories-42608302.

"Nepal woman and children die in banned 'menstruation hut'." *British Broadcasting Corporation*, January 10, 2019, https://www.bbc.com/news/world-asia-46823289.

Quine, W.V.O. "Posits and Reality." In *Ways of Paradox and Other Essays*, Kingsport: Random House, 1966.

Quran. Tanzil.net, http://tanzil.net.

Saafi, Michael. "'I'm born to do this': Condemned by caste, India's sewer cleaners risk death daily." *The Guardian*, March 04, 2018, https://www.theguardian.com/world/2018/mar/04/im-born-to-do-this-condemned-by-caste-indias-sewer-cleaners-risk-death-daily.

Stacke, Sarah. "The Risky Lives of Women Sent Into Exile—For Menstruating." National Geographic, March 10, 2017, https://www.nationalgeographic.com/photography/proof/2017/03/menstruation-rituals-nepal/.

Tafażżolī , Aḥmad. *Encyclopaedia Iranica, Online Edition*, s.v. "Činwad Puhl." December 15, 1991, v.5,

http://www.iranicaonline.org/articles/cinwad-puhl-av.

The Bhagavad Gītā Twenty-fi fth-Anniversary Edition. Edited by Christopher Key Chappel. Translated by Winthrop Sargeant. New York: State University of New York Press, 2009.

The Complete Tanakh (Tanach) - Hebrew Bible with Rashi's commentary. Translated and edited by Rabbi A.J. Rosenberg. chabad.org, https://www.chabad.org/library/bible_cdo/aid/63255/jewish/The-Bible-with-Rashi.htm.

The Holy Bible, New King James Version. The Gideons International, 1985.

The Holy Quran. Translated and Annotated by S.V. Mir Ahmed Ali, Mirza Mahdi Pooya Yazdi. Tehran: Osweh Printing and Publication Co., 1988.

The Laws of Manu. Edited by G. Buhler. Oxford: The Clarendon Press, 1886.

The Law of Non-Contradiction: New Philosophical Essays. Edited by Graham Priest, J.C. Beall, and Bradley Armour-Garb. New York: Oxford University Press, 2004.

Wendy Doniger. *On Hinduism.* New York: Oxford University Press, 2014.